Renegotiate with Integrity

"It's not business, it's personal."

"I am pleased to tell you that Marc's book is excellent. I have reviewed many negotiation books and this one I can highly recommend to my clients. What sets his book apart from others is that the negotiation advice is very realistic, unlike many academic negotiation publications. It also covers a very important field of negotiation (renegotiation) that is not widely written about. Although he doesn't use the standard academic terminology for certain negotiation behaviors, he is accurate in his descriptions and usage of the strategies and tactics. His writing style and examples are very engaging. I thoroughly enjoyed the book."

Holly Schroth, Ph.D., Senior Lecturer,
Haas School of Business, University of California, Berkeley

"When it comes to renegotiation, Marc is simply the very best. He renegotiated $140 million worth of equipment, carrier, and fiber contracts for my international telecommunications company in late 2000 and early 2001. He did this with such integrity and clarity that vendors actually felt good after the final settlement."

Dr. Christopher W. Hartnett, Chairman, USA Global Link

"If you are in deals that you need to alter due to changed circumstances, you *must* read this book. Marc has presented a real-life approach to allow the reader to take his system and put it immediately into action."

Ron Shapiro and Mark Jankowski, authors of
'The Power of Nice' and 'Bullies, Tyrants, and Impossible People.'

"Unlike other writers about negotiation, Marc Freeman has the self-confidence—and class—to tell us what he has learned from his failures as well as his successes."

Steven P. Cohen, President, The Negotiation Skills Company.

"A week after the workshop I discovered that my attitude had altered to the point where I was able to participate with tolerance, strength, and humor, in a conflict involving three different companies. What a change!"

Samantha Wallace, Independent Writer

"I thoroughly enjoyed the renegotiating workshop with Marc Freeman. Marc really helped me see everything clearly and get the results my business needs. Even the other parties were satisfied after talking with him!"

Lonica Halley, Owner, Natural Selections

"Marc Freeman has a deep understanding of what it takes to get two sides to work out their differences in an ethical way. I recommend his workshop wholeheartedly to anyone who wants to become better at the business of life."

Ronald B. Stakland, CEO, SoilSoup, Inc.

"I found Marc's seminar highly informative, with many useful points for any business or individual. I implemented some of Marc's principles the very next day with great success."

Carl Stone, Real Estate Investor

"This workshop is a *must do* for lawyers. Marc's workshop gives us important tools for resolving conflicts and reaching solutions that serve our client and our client's relationships."

Len Labagh, Attorney

Renegotiate with Integrity

"It's not business, it's personal."

Marc Freeman

Freeman Business Books
A Division of Freeman Publishing
Fairfield, Iowa USA

Publisher Cataloging in Publication Data:
Freeman, Marc
Renegotiate with integrity : it's not business, it's personal / Marc Freeman
ISBN 1-4276-0852-0
1. Renegotiation
2. Business
3. Self-Help

Visit Freeman Publishing at www.renegotiate.tv.
Book design by Concept Interface (www.acobb.com).
Cover design by Josie Hannes Design (www.jhannesdesign.com).
Cover photo by Rick Donhauser.
Printed in the United States of America.

FOR MARCI

I dedicate this book to Marci, my wife, and to our three children, Jonathan, Leela, and Eliana, who continue to amaze me with their deep level of understanding of who they are and who they want to be. My love and respect for them is immeasurable. I have to give all four of these wonderful people credit for raising me from a very young man to a very young older man.

TABLE OF CONTENTS

Dedication   v

Foreword by Herb Cohen   ix

Introduction   xiii

Chapter 1 - The Critical Path   1

Chapter 2 - The Secret of the Orange Ball   51

Chapter 3 - Hit the Refresh Button   93

Chapter 4 - Transcend the Details   123

Chapter 5 - Call in the Cavalry   139

Chapter 6 - The Seven Fundamentals.   165

Chapter 7 - Applying the Principles.   211

Appendix A - Recommended Reading   243

Appendix B - Workbook   245

Appendix C - About the Author   259

Acknowledgements   261

Index   267

Foreword

In most of the world, negotiating is an art form—intricate as a ballroom dance, expressive as a Picasso painting, and as affirming as scoring the winning goal in a World Cup football game.

In the United States, however, as evidenced by growing trade imbalances, budget deficits, increasing civil litigation, and dissatisfaction with international dealings, we have had problems with doing the dance and playing the game.

Still, for each of us, dealing with differences or conflict is a ubiquitous activity that adjusts and transforms relationships. It occurs when two or more parties attempt to merge their disparate points of view into a single resolution. If successful, all sides prefer the agreed outcome to the status quo (*i.e.*, no agreement) or any other mutually acceptable outcomes.

This is where Marc Freeman (the author of this new book) really shines. He has the willingness and experience to help parties adjust or rearrange their future relationships. In short, he is a modern day "rainmaker" who can transform chaos into cosmos.

Marc emphasizes the word *re*-negotiate, implying that the parties have had some sort of prior affiliation which has been jeopardized as a result of change. Thus he attempts to reorder a *new* combination of common and conflicting interests.

So for him "renegotiating" is not a contest of wills, involving payoff demands and manipulative maneuvers designed to maximize one's interest at the expense of the other side.

To the contrary, Marc sees renegotiation as a dynamic problem-solving process, whereby both sides interact to share their real preferences, needs, and interests so that mutually acceptable exchanges can be made. The result: agreements that bring "value added" dimensions to the relationship.

It has been almost three decades since I wrote *You Can Negotiate Anything,* a book that has sold almost three million copies and has been translated into twenty-six languages. Since then more than 1,500 different articles and books have been published devoted to this subject.

Amid this abundance, what is especially unique about *Renegotiate with Integrity?* First of all, it is a highly readable work that is both lively and provocative. Since the author's attitude and spirit flows through his pen or word processor it has the aroma of authenticity and honesty.

Secondly, one can easily identify with Marc's illuminating stories and examples. Actually, I tend to admire him for his humility, generosity, and willingness to share credit.

Finally, the author takes on the sacred American legalistic concept that a contract, once signed, is absolutely binding. This view holds that, in essence, even though subsequent unanticipated events may cause an injustice to one side, all parties are still required to comply literally with all the terms of the contract.

Marc, on the other hand (along with most of the rest of the world), understands that an agreement can and should be revisited as changes occur. He is very much in the Far Eastern tradition, which holds that even after a contract has been executed it can be revisited when and if compliance or changes in pay-off occur.

Marc Freeman's approach elegantly transforms the classic Japanese ethic, that rules should be modified and adjusted if they run counter to human needs, into a simple and practical approach for the modern world. In the end, "There's always a law beyond a law to render justice."

November 2006
Herb Cohen

Introduction

Negotiating is a necessary part of life. Most of us don't realize how often we negotiate deals and relationships. But *renegotiating* is even more tightly woven into the fabric of our lives than negotiating itself is.

Renegotiating is the art of altering, revising, or changing a previously negotiated relationship. This relationship can be in the form of any professional or personal contract or commitment involving a written or oral promise.

But what is it really? Plainly stated, renegotiating is reneging on a promise or commitment. What do we think of people who don't keep their promises or commitments? Not very much.

Nevertheless, I contend that *we can renegotiate with integrity.* We can renegotiate successfully and keep our reputation intact—whether we're the ones who must break a commitment, or the ones on the receiving end of a broken commitment.

Every day we act within a complex, sometimes conflicting, web of personal, business, and professional relationships. How do we keep them all moving in the right direction? We *renegotiate* them—all the time! All successful relationships are sustained through renegotiation.

Elka Altbach, a good friend of mine, is a professional mediator. When she heard I was writing this book, she told me she was glad someone was finally defining the concept of renegotiation. It is Elka's experience that there are two main points every negotiator must understand and communicate to all parties *before* they sign a contract:

1. *There are some portions of* any *contract that may have to be renegotiated.* No matter where you may be in the process of negotiating an agreement, it should be clearly understood *from the beginning* that this is a fluid world and things will change. If this understanding exists at the start of the negotiation, it will be an invaluable help later when change inevitably occurs.

2. *The need to renegotiate a deal does not mean the original negotiation was a failure.* Again, things always change. It is a given that most deals will probably not remain completely satisfactory for both parties for the duration of the contract. And if the contract is a problem for one party, then it is a problem for the other. Renegotiating is an ideal response in most instances.

When I brought out these points in one of my recent workshops, a lawyer stood up and told us that this was precisely why he tried to leave some ambiguity in every contract he writes. This is how he leaves an opening for renegotiating.

It's Nothing New

Most of us have been renegotiating our whole lives. We did it with our parents when we were growing up. When we became parents we did it with our children: "I know I promised to take you shopping today, but something came up. Tell you what, let's go tomorrow instead, and I'll take you to lunch too." Ever heard that one?

How about: "Dad, I know I agreed not to go out Saturday night so I could spend time with the family, but that was before I found out about this party. If you let me go, I'll stay home the next two Saturday nights."

Or this one from work: "I know I missed the deadline, but give me another two days and you won't be disappointed, I promise." In daily life, renegotiating is a given.

How are negotiating and renegotiating alike? They both deal with the dynamics involved in moving two or more parties towards an agreement, contract, or promise.

How do they differ? Every renegotiation is a follow-up to a previously existing agreement. A renegotiation has a history; a negotiation usually does not. This distinction holds the key to understanding how to renegotiate.

First, let's admit that renegotiating is, indeed, reneging on a promise or agreement we've made. This starting point gives us the right perspective on what we're attempting to do when we renegotiate. We shouldn't fool ourselves into thinking that we are *not* breaking or changing a promise or commitment. This is why the *approach* is so critical.

Don't ever try and "spin" this perspective. It won't work, and it's not honest. Be clear about what you're doing when you want to re-negotiate, and you will be received more positively. We don't have to feel guilty that we can't keep our promise. Feeling guilty is a waste of time. Renegotiating is inevitable *because things change.*

How could we possibly keep every promise we've ever made? It's impossible. So don't worry about it. Just understand renegotiating for what it is: an opportunity to change a relationship that is no longer working.

We may need to renegotiate due to a variety of factors. Any of them could lead us to revisit a previous commitment and find out whether or not it still fits—and will continue to fit—our needs. Change can be a friend or an enemy. I learned an old saying when I was working in China: "You either learn to ride the tiger, or be eaten by it."

It's an easy assumption that once we make a promise, or sign a con-tract, everyone on both sides will stick to it. The common wisdom is that a person who tries to get out of such an obligation lacks integrity, but this is not necessarily so. I will show you that you can, and should, renegotiate when necessary, and with complete honesty and integrity (hence the title of this book).

Changing circumstances are what usually cause us to break prom-ises and lead us to renegotiate our commitments. On the basis of this understanding, let's investigate the practical principles, tools, and insights of renegotiating. I've formulated five principles that have helped me immensely, and which will help you view renegoti-ating in a new light:

> ## Freeman's Five Principles of Renegotiating
>
> 1. **The Critical Path**
>
> 2. **Secret of the Orange Ball**
>
> 3. **Hit the Refresh Button**
>
> 4. **Transcend the Details**
>
> 5. **Call in the Cavalry**

What Will You Learn from this Book?

The chapters of this book are arranged according to the five principles, followed by a guide to renegotiating and a review of specific renegotiation examples.

1. The Critical Path

Chapter one establishes how to begin: how to organize a renegotiation on the basis of proper behavior. We identify the milestones that structure the natural sequence of any successful renegotiation:

Common Ground, Plausible Solution, Comfort Zone, and Settlement. These four milestones tell us where we are at any point in the renegotiation process and how we're proceeding. We then examine a checklist of ten specific keys to a successful renegotiation.

2. The Secret of the Orange Ball

Chapter two presents a set of techniques to identify who is in control of the renegotiation process at any particular time, and how to *take* control to reach the next stage. We use the image of the Orange Ball as a symbol for control—whoever holds the Orange Ball is in control of the process.

3. Hit the Refresh Button

Chapter three explains some key techniques for keeping all parties (yourself included) focused on the real goals at hand. The techniques described in this chapter operate on the basis of keeping and getting control of the Orange Ball.

4. Transcend the Details

Chapter four focuses on getting through each stage of the renegotiation without getting bogged down in the details.

5. Call in the Cavalry

Chapter five will help you decide when and where to look for help during a renegotiation, and how to make best use of the valuable experience and expertise that others can offer you. Access to a third party's objective perspective can be critical to creating a settlement.

6. The Seven Fundamentals of Renegotiating

Chapter six covers the basics of what to do, and how to behave, in any renegotiating situation. Frequently referring back to these seven fundamentals will keep you on track.

7. Applying the Principles

Chapter seven reviews all the principles in the context of specific types of contracts and agreements. I've identified five basic types of relationships that might require some kind of renegotiation, with examples of how the five principles work within each type:

1. real estate lease renegotiations and buyouts
2. contract renegotiations and buyouts
3. contract collections
4. restructuring debt (accounts payable / accounts receivable)
5. personal contracts

We'll investigate why some renegotiations work and some don't. Then we'll show you how to make the best of a bad situation, and how to proceed if there is antagonism or anger on both sides. In many cases, neither the company nor the customer has done anything wrong, yet the relationship between them is no longer viable for one or both of them. This can occur for a variety of reasons, which we'll discuss at length. We'll also look at the many different types of relationships that may be renegotiated.

Looking Forward

I'm a professional *renegotiator*. You won't find the word in the dictionary. I use it because *"renegotiator"* expresses precisely what everyone becomes when they need to change a promise or commitment.

While I've been writing this book, it's become clear to me that I have been renegotiating since childhood. And over the years, more often than not, I have found myself renegotiating on behalf of others. I've never been happy knowing that one of my friends or family members was treated unfairly or taken advantage of by any company or individual. And I've never been afraid to try to straighten out the situation.

I've successfully renegotiated hundreds of millions of dollars worth of contracts all over the world, and—heaven knows—with a wife of 32 years and three grown children, I've also done my share of personal renegotiating.

My stories illustrate how I have both succeeded and failed in these renegotiations. Hopefully, you'll learn what works and what doesn't.

This is not an academic book of theory; the dates, timing, and numbers in these stories are approximations based on my best recollection. This is a practical book, filled with real examples of what I've learned to be the most effective tools for creating successful renegotiations.

My approach to renegotiating is based on the firmly held conviction that *everyone* can learn to renegotiate successfully, and with integrity. In fact, I believe that everyone *must* learn to renegotiate with integrity. If we have to break our promises or commitments, let's learn to do it right. And when promises or commitments to us are broken, let's behave properly: with insight, forethought, and compassion. It works both ways.

A lot of people in my workshops have told me that my approach to teaching successful renegotiating is simply showing people how to treat one another respectfully—and it's true. One of the things I like to do is remind my clients of something they already know, but often forget: *Always treat yourself and others with respect.*

Renegotiating with integrity requires clear and honest communication between all parties. Approach is crucial. If our approach to the other party is honest, direct, and humble (yes, humble! and I will explain why later), our chance of a positive response is much higher. *Treating people with respect is the first key to successful renegotiating.*

There are lots of books about negotiating, and I've read most of them. Actually—because telling the truth is one of the most important points of negotiating and renegotiating—I should say that I have *skimmed* these books. I have read enough to know that almost everything has already been written about negotiating. Very little, however, has been written about *renegotiating,* which in my experience occurs far more often.

Who Should Read this Book?

Business executives, managers, sales people, buyers, customer service associates, human resource managers, husbands, wives, and students: anyone who wants to improve professional or personal relationships.

> *The ultimate goal in any renegotiation is to find a comfort zone that both parties can live with, and which will lead to a settlement.*

> *Being right is not the issue.*
> *Win-Win is not the issue.*
> *Being fair is not even always the issue.*

> *Being honest, up-front, direct, flexible, and respectful is the issue —*
> *and will help you find a common ground that will lead to a successful settlement.*

What does it take to be a good renegotiator? Be a good listener, be nice, be honest, flexible, and creative. It also helps to use humor when appropriate. But most of all, I am convinced that we can accomplish much more in our lives if we just treat each other with respect. If our behavior reflects how we would like to be treated, we will be more successful in every endeavor. These are simple, powerful points that we can use in all aspects of our lives.

In my opinion it's time for business people to consider the human element in our dealings—the *personal* effect of our actions on others in our professional and personal relationships. We have to start taking full responsibility for ourselves, for all our actions and their effects. Why? Because, *"It's not business, it's personal."*

I'm not being simplistic, I'm just being real. Of course, there *are* a lot of people who say you can't use this approach in business because people will take advantage of you.

My response is, I don't care and I don't believe it. The point of this book is that it's possible *and it's necessary* for us to keep our personal integrity, our character, and our good reputation, while we are doing business. And when we bring these attributes into our personal lives, we're rewarded many times over.

Here is why *It's not business, it's personal*:

1. *All of our interactions are with people.* Relationships of every kind and in every situation—even those between large corporations or countries—are conducted person-to-person. When we recognize this fact, we are already on the right track.

2. *Our reputation is personal.* (If it isn't, it should be.) So many times I hear business people say, while they are cheating or mistreating someone, "Listen, I like you. This isn't personal. It's just business." Then they laugh because they think they're being clever. What they don't understand is that our actions reflect who we are and what we are. Our actions create our reputation. It's *very* personal! A lot of people spin the truth to justify their actions. But if our actions affect those we're dealing with, then by definition, it *is* personal.

3. In every situation we encounter, *we can choose how we behave.* There have been times in my business life when I chose expediency over doing the right thing—cutting corners to save time and money, or not considering other people's needs. I'm not proud of this. My reputation has

always been important to me and I learned a long time ago that if I want to maintain a good reputation, then I have to pay attention to my behavior.

Remember, *always behave as if it's personal but react as if it's business.* If you do, your rate of success will increase dramatically. This stance will enable you to be more objective, while at the same time it constantly reminds you to behave with respect and integrity.

Throughout this book, we'll be emphasizing approach in all our discussion of renegotiation. If you approach a renegotiation properly, you might even end up with a friend instead of an adversary.

Some years back, I was hired to renegotiate one contract that was felt to be utterly impossible to get out of. It wasn't working and it was a waste of money for my client—a web-based advertising company called Mypoints.

Mypoints had to get out of the deal for a variety of reasons. The contract was with a company called Storage Networks, which sold digital storage. But the contract was rock solid, and my client did have the money to pay. Why should Storage Networks allow Mypoints to get out of a contract that was producing profitable revenue for them?

Mypoints had spent months dealing with Storage Networks at every level of the company, trying to get them to work out a deal. They finally decided to turn over the renegotiations to me and I began to pursue a solution.

My contact at Storage Networks was Christine McKay, and since I use her story later in the book, I won't go into the details now, but we worked together over a period of weeks to come up with a solution that was equitable for both sides. By the time the deal was settled, we had become good friends.

Now, how could a solid friendship come about in what appeared to be an adversarial situation? From the beginning, Christine realized that I wasn't trying to get my client out of the contract at the expense of her company's needs. I was willing to convince my client to be fair. And I realized early on that Christine, while completely loyal to her company's position, was willing to listen to any fair solution. On this basis, our professional and personal friendship developed. (Christine has since left her employer and become one of the best negotiators and renegotiators I know.)

This brings up something that constantly bothers me: why do we behave differently at work than we do in our personal lives? Many of us feel we can't let down and be ourselves at work because it's not "professional." This pressure to change our personalities and behavior when we are at work creates a strain on our physiology and well-being. This strain creates stress, which in turn can, and often does, lead to illness. On the other hand, there is the additional danger of bringing our work behavior into the home, and treating our family like our co-workers, or even worse, like our employees. It's not a healthy situation.

We have the power to change, and this book will endeavor to help you do just that.

Before we get started, I want to tell you three astonishing things:

1. You won't always agree with me.

2. I won't always be right.

3. You may find contradictory statements throughout this book. This is because life is full of contradictions.

CHAPTER ONE

The Critical Path

What is a critical path and how does it apply to renegotiating? I wouldn't take a trip across the county without first looking at a map. I try to identify the larger cities along the way, and then I double-check that I have everything with me that I need for the trip.

Every renegotiation is like a trip. I've identified four major landmarks (the Critical Path) and I've provided a checklist of ten key things to do (the Renegotiation Checklist): five before you get started, and five along the way.

The Great Spin

Before you get into the Critical Path, and before you renegotiate anything for anyone, ask yourself this question: what are my real intentions, my real goals? If you can clearly and honestly define your intentions, and the intentions of the people you represent, your ability to move the other side to an agreement increases manyfold. But if being right is what's important to you, you'll be in for

the struggle of your life. In most situations, there is a big difference between honestly defining your intentions, and the desire to
be right. Don't worry about being right—it's not what it's cracked
up to be.

As human beings, we enjoy that quality which sets us apart from
other species—free will. But the notion of free will seems to have
become muddied in re-
cent years, to include
what I call the Great
Spin. We use the Great
Spin to justify anything
we do, from theft to war.

FREEMAN'S FIVE PRINCIPLES

1. The Critical Path

*You must follow the Critical Path
to renegotiate successfully.*

Why do we try to justify
our worst actions? Is it to
make us look good in the
eyes of others? No, it's to make us look good in our own eyes. We
try to convince ourselves that if we're armed with good intentions,
then our consequent actions—right or wrong—are "justified" by
circumstances. This is why people can say, "it's not personal, it's
just business." This is dangerous territory.

> *Don't ever spin the truth (even to yourself),
> or allow your clients to spin the truth,
> in order to justify a particular position.*

Let's take an example: You can no longer afford your rent, and your
landlord has a solid lease that he expects you to abide by. What do
you do? If you ask to get out of the lease, you cannot justify your
request by saying, "I'm in the right." And you shouldn't spin your

story to make yourself right. It won't work because your landlord will probably get angry and stick to his legal rights. On the other hand, if you're honest with the landlord and explain why you can't afford the space, then you may well get his help.

People tend to want to help one another if they see a legitimate need. When we act in an honest and straightforward way, we inspire others to do the same. It may not be in the landlord's financial interest to help you out, but he may very well do it anyway because it's the right thing to do.

Most of us tend to spin stories to make ourselves "right," to put our situation in a better light. The spin is about justification. On some level, though, people can tell when you're not being honest. They can smell a spin. In everyday life they may not confront you with it, but it will almost always come out in the course of negotiation and renegotiation.

I had an early lesson in understanding the difference between spinning the story to create a particular position, and the real facts that I needed to communicate.

My first boss, Sal Bonavito, CEO of Coffee Imports International, always wanted information about what was happening in our marketplace. I was his salesman for Northern California and I loved collecting information. When I first began giving Sal news of what was going on with stores, buyers and products, I used to elaborate and give my opinion as well.

He told me to stop doing this. He wanted the information unfiltered so that he could use it to improve our company. He always asked for my opinion afterwards, but he did not want me to spin a story before I gave him the *real* information. It sounds easy to give unfiltered information, but it isn't.

Remember the TV show *Dragnet*: "Just the facts, ma'am." In renegotiating, even more than in negotiating, it's critical that you don't spin the facts. Spinning is the best way to get the whole process off-track, to get *off* the Critical Path.

The Critical Path — Four Stages

Every renegotiation can be broken down into four stages. Each stage is a milestone, like a critical destination that you must reach in order to move forward to the next one. Some milestones you might just drive past, while at others you might have to stop and spend a few days or weeks.

1. Common Ground. The first milestone is where the goals, needs, and expectations of the two sides intersect. Basically, this is where both sides agree that there is an opportunity to settle differences, and that they are willing to renegotiate.

2. Plausible Solution. On the basis of the Common Ground, you will find the Plausible Solution—often a *pair* of potential resolutions (one for each party) with considerable overlap that both parties can probably live with. In many cases, the solution lies in what each party states it's willing to do to create a settlement.

3. Comfort Zone. The Plausible Solution then gives rise to the Comfort Zone—the limits within which each side feels comfortable, and beyond which they will not go. Usually this has to do with money and timing. How much is each side willing to accept in order to settle? The Comfort Zone can also be the stage for deciding when and how the money is transferred and how long the new agreement should last.

There may also be a point where one side has concluded they just need to move on. It's common for one side or the other to feel that enough time and energy have been spent, and they've just had enough and don't want to continue with the process.

4. Settlement.   Once the Comfort Zone is established, it's time to move right on to the Settlement. This is where you put the details of the Comfort Zone into a written agreement. I usually hire a lawyer to write up or review the Settlement.

The Critical Path

Common Ground

➔ *Plausible Solution*

➔ *Comfort Zone*

➔ *Settlement*

The following simple sequence is the most concise guide I can come up with to help you stay on course throughout every renegotiation:

The Common Ground gives rise to the Plausible Solution.

The Comfort Zone produces the Settlement.

When you understand these two fundamental relationships, you have grasped the essence of renegotiating.

From the Common Ground to the Comfort Zone

There are many ways to create a settlement. Right and wrong are not issues here. The only real issue is: can both parties accept the outcome? In other words, are they ready to answer the question, "How do we move on?"

Moving on means everyone gets to put their time, energy, and creativity into building the company, creating profit, and focusing on new business. Everyone involved must recognize the huge cost when resources of time, money, and company psychology are spent on negative issues. Years of experience have taught me that *moving on* is the basis for every Common Ground, and it should be the major goal for both sides in any renegotiation.

Finding the Common Ground does not have to be difficult. Many times it's right in front of you, but it just takes time to see it.

At one point, I was renegotiating our company's rates with a large hotel chain. The hotel group had a formula, based on the number of nights a company committed to for a year. My job was to change that "formula thinking" so I could get the best deal, regardless of how many nights we stayed. The problem was how to get the hotel officials to a position, or a Comfort Zone, where they could make the decision we wanted.

First, I had to establish the Common Ground. This meant the hotel management had to acknowledge their commitment to keeping our company as a customer—which we of course wanted as well. Once that Common Ground was established, moving on to the Comfort Zone would be much easier.

I did get the hotel management to say they really wanted to find a way to keep us. They admitted we were a good customer and they liked having us stay throughout the year. With three to five people traveling at any given time, we had spent 75 nights in their hotel chain the previous year. Now this isn't a big number, but it wasn't small either. A good (and savvy) company cherishes the type of customer who not only gives them repeat business but would also recommend them to other companies.

At this point in the renegotiation, I had to create a Plausible Solution. And I had to find a compelling reason for the hotel to move from their standard formula so I could get the kind of discount I wanted. They urged me to go out and shop it around, and find out what the competition would offer me.

I called some other hotel chains which, when they heard my current deal, were willing to do better, a lot better. I went back to the original chain and told them other hotel chains were offering me a better deal—and with no requirement for extra nights.

I said, "You're forcing me to move." Although I had many reasons for not moving to another chain, I was willing to move if we couldn't come to an agreement. At this point, the hotel management came around and gave me the deal that I wanted because they had a compelling reason to do so. I had created their Plausible Solution for them. Their Solution was to give me the discount I requested; the Comfort Zone would establish the size of the discount by moving away from their standard rates.

I had established my own Comfort Zone early on: I wanted better rates, including breakfast, and when available, upgrades to the executive floor or better rooms at a specific rate. This offer, or Comfort Zone, was always on the table for them to accept. I just had to give them a reason to feel OK accepting it. After we found the Common Ground and Solution, they were comfortable taking a good look at my Comfort Zone to see if they could accept this as well. Once they did, the settlement details were put in writing and we signed an agreement with very few adjustments. (There are always small adjustments to the Comfort Zone when you put it in writing to create the Final Settlement.)

The Comfort Zone Isn't the Settlement

Let's look at the difference between the Comfort Zone and the actual Settlement. The two may seem to be the same, but that's not necessarily so.

> *The Comfort Zone sets the ground rules*
> *for achieving the final Settlement.*

The Settlement requires that all the details of the Comfort Zone be in place. You may have deals in which you have established a strong Common Ground and Plausible Solution, and have also created an agreeable Comfort Zone, but then you get bogged down when you try to put everything in writing in the Settlement agreement.

I usually have a lawyer review this document just to make sure that I've adequately protected my client's interests. (Deals often become more complicated when lawyers try to put all the details in writing.) Your attorney's job is to make sure that you are protected if things go wrong. The precise wording is very important because it should describe exactly how you and the other side must perform in order to achieve the details of the Comfort Zone.

For example, in the story above, one of the reasons the management liked us as a customer was because we used the hotel during the off-season. And even though both sides had agreed on a Comfort Zone, when it came time to write up the agreement, the hotel wanted us to agree to stay for a minimum number of nights during the off season. They didn't want us to use all our nights when they were busiest and the hotel would be full at higher rates anyway. I didn't want to commit in writing to an off-season minimum, but I understood their position and agreed to include it.

We actually didn't use lawyers to write up this particular agreement. It was a simple document and didn't require legal expertise. Also, there were no legal ramifications if we did not fulfill the agreement. The hotel could just take away our special rates.

Whether or not lawyers are involved, the details have to be worked out based on the already-established Comfort Zone. Without the Comfort Zone you can never finish the Settlement and move on.

The Settlement Is Not Always Fair

It's important to understand from the outset of any renegotiation that the settlement may not be fair, especially when money is involved. This is why it's critical to remember: *It's not business, it's personal.* No matter which side of the renegotiation you're on, someone usually feels he paid too much and someone usually feels he received too little. Rarely does the settlement amount turn out to be just right for both sides.

What is the right amount? There is an easy answer: it's the amount each side is comfortable with—the amount that creates the Comfort Zone in order to *move on*. It's often much more important to move on than to continue dickering about money. And being honest with people and showing them respect takes a surprising amount of the sting out of losing money.

I want to tell you two stories that illustrate how the settlement amount may not always be fair.

Something Is Better than Nothing

At one time my responsibilities at the telecom company I worked for included reorganizing their accounts payable. Many companies in the telecom industry had terrible billing and collection practices, and even poorer reconciliation responses. We owed several hundred thousand dollars to the carrier that offered the least expensive route for our Brazil traffic, although we were still selling the route and getting paid from our customers. But because the carrier refused to reconcile our account, we hadn't been able to pay them for months.

In other words, there were many calls on our invoice that had not been made through us, and it was up to the carrier to sort them out. In addition, we were trying to establish that we should not have to pay for dropped or unanswered calls.

When the carrier called us for the money, we told them that they hadn't reconciled our account, which was true—we owed them less than was on their books. And we knew if we paid them what they were asking, they would *never* reconcile our account. By not paying their invoice we forced them to do the reconciliation.

According to our records, we owed them close to $150,000, but according to their books we owed almost $500,000. In the end, even though our number proved correct, we still weren't able pay them in full. We decided that the best thing we could do was to cancel the service and not incur any more debt.

I offered them $10,000 a month for four months. Was this fair? Absolutely not. But it was the best that we could do at the time, and if they didn't accept it they could end up getting nothing. They asked for $10,000 a month for six months. I told them that even four months was stretching it for us; I was sure we could make three payments, and I had added a month just to try and help out. They didn't like it at all. But what could they do?

They knew that during this difficult time they might end up with nothing, so their Comfort Zone had to be within a wide range of numbers. They were simply trying to get as much as they could before we went under. Furthermore, at this time they had larger receivables with other companies that they needed to focus on.

My responsibility to my company was to conserve as much cash as I could. And our policy was, as much as possible, to pay the companies that supplied us with the routes for which we were being paid by our customers. In bankruptcies, or when companies are closing down, smaller companies usually receive almost nothing. We took the opposite approach. The carrier company ended up settling for the four months with the understanding that the fourth month might not happen.

The company provided us with good service at a good price. I was direct and completely honest with them, and they received what money there was, more quickly than if the company had filed for bankruptcy. They had reconciled our account on time, as they should have, or they certainly would not have been paid in full. Nevertheless, the company got our receivables off their books and could move on to invest their time and energy in other projects.

The downturn in the telecom industry resulted in hard times for many companies. This is a fact, not an excuse. Fortunately, because we handled our accounts responsibly, we were one of the few telecom companies not to file for bankruptcy. We found a settlement that may not have been in their Comfort Zone, but at least it was something. Maybe we should call these situations "Uncomfortable Zones."

> *The opportunity to move on*
> *is the goal of every renegotiation.*

Perpetual Renegotiation

When I used to sell to department stores, there were always significant deductions on our invoices for various reasons. Department stores often took deductions for infractions by the vendor. They also frequently deducted more for advertising than the amount originally agreed upon with the vendor.

In the industry we called these situations "deduct and discuss," because there was never an opportunity, prior to the deduction, to talk to the store about the problems or infractions. For that matter, it was rare for a store *ever* to discuss the deductions at all. And when we did challenge the store, we could never find the right person to verify that the deduction was incorrect and, therefore, taken improperly. We never managed to get our "day in court." As a result, we always had to figure in a few percentage points for these deductions.

On the other hand, overcharging for advertising was something we could renegotiate. Advertising dollars for stores are usually calculated as a certain percentage of what the store buys. For example, if the store purchases $100,000 worth of merchandise and the advertising budget is ten percent, then they could legitimately deduct $10,000 from their invoice as the advertising expense.

But frequently what happened was that buyers would "agree" to order $100,000 worth of merchandise so that they could get the $10,000 advertising deduction. Then the actual order would come in for only—let's say—$70,000, but they would still deduct $10,000 rather than the correct amount of $7,000.

When the store deducted more for advertising than what was earned, I had to call the buyer and ask how the deduction amount had been calculated. The buyer would always make the excuse that the deduction taken was the amount that we had agreed upon when the purchase was made. This was a game because the buyer knew very well what the deal really was, and that the store had not earned the deducted amount. What was important was to take the time to go through the points.

I would set up a meeting with the buyer to show the paperwork and explain that the number they could deduct was based on a percentage of the purchase orders. If the buyer ordered less than the specified amount, the advertising deduction went down proportionately. Inevitably, the buyers would plead innocence, and I couldn't say anything. I had to play ball if I wanted to keep them as customers.

I needed to figure out how to deal with this mess. Most of the time, buyers would buy their way out. In other words, they would place another order to cover the additional amount of the deduction. This wasn't fair, but if I intended to continue doing business with them I had to accept it. Buyers would never just cut a check and pay me back what they owed. If I demanded a check, I could conceivably get it from them, but then they probably would never buy from me again. The retail business is tough, so before I went in to meet with the buyer I had to decide very clearly what my Comfort Zone was going to be.

Believe it or not, it's important not to be attached to having a fair Settlement. There are more important things. It *is* important to be able to move on from a deal that is wasting time and money, and raising your blood pressure, to deals that will be profitable. Sometimes it's better just to walk away than to push for the extra dollar.

Once you feel you've gotten as much as there is to get, that's going to have to be your Comfort Zone. Settle the deal and move on. If you push too hard, it can backfire. The other party will walk away and you will end up getting nothing.

*The line between getting as much
as you can and nothing is very fine.
Pay attention to it.*

Being Right Is Not Always the Issue

Early in any renegotiation you will usually discover which party is in the right. Most of the time, it simply doesn't matter. When it *does* matter, then you may have the opportunity to be indignant.

Let me tell you a funny story. Since he found out that I was writing this book, my friend Len Oppenheim has been telling me story after story about his renegotiating experiences. Every time we play golf, he says, "I have another story you should put in your book." Here's one that's worth telling.

In the middle of the summer, Len was traveling with his family and had arranged to rent a car at O'Hare airport from one of the major rental companies. The flights were all messed up, so by the time he reached the rental counter at O'Hare he was tired, but since he was a VIP member he was at least glad that there wouldn't be any hassle getting a car.

As usual, the rental company was great and the car was ready to go with no waiting. Len and his family began to drive to their friends' house in the Chicago suburbs.

An hour out of O'Hare they noticed that the air conditioning was no longer working. They would be using the car for a full week, and at this time of year air conditioning was essential. He pulled over and noticed that they were near a small airport, in Palwaukee.

Len called the rental company and asked if they rented cars out of Palwaukee.

They said they did, so he decided to go to their Palwaukee rental office and exchange cars.

When he got to the car counter he was informed that they didn't have any available cars and would not have any for several more days. Len called the national customer service line again and explained his problem: the air conditioning had broken down 30 miles from O'Hare and the Palwaukee office did not have any cars.

Calmly, he suggested that he leave the car parked in front of his friend's house for a few days, thereby giving the company 48 hours to replace the defective car.

The national agent said they didn't do that and Len would have to go back to O'Hare himself to replace the car.

Len felt his request was quite reasonable and he had offered them a very workable solution. He did not want to drag his family back to O'Hare and get another car as it was close to the commute hour; it would take another two hours to get to his friend's house.

The agent was firm and said they just didn't do what Len had suggested.

Len said, "Fine. Either you replace the car in Glencoe or I will drive the car right into Lake Michigan. It's the only way I can cool it off."

The agent was taken aback and she said there was really nothing she could do, "But maybe you should speak to my supervisor."

"All right," Len responded, "I'm giving you or your supervisor five minutes to come up with a solution that satisfies me, or the car is going into the lake."

Within five minutes a supervisor called back to say that they had arranged for a car to be freed up right there in Palwaukee. So Len got a new car with air conditioning that worked, and continued on his way.

Only use these threatening tactics as a very last resort; they can often backfire.

This story has nothing to do with whether or not Len was right. From his side it was all about "being in the right." Not only right, but also making a very reasonable suggestion as a solution to the situation.

The car rental agency didn't care about that. They had a policy and they wanted to stick to it. But Len gave them no other choice but to accommodate his request. He was dead serious about driving the car into the lake. (I know him: he would have done it.) He believed the car rental company wouldn't want the publicity and the whole situation would make them look stupid. Besides, their policy made no sense. He was not going to accept anything less than satisfaction. The Comfort Zone for the car rental company was that they didn't want one of their cars ending up in a lake.

I would like to bring together all of the geniuses who create policies for these large companies and give them one big lesson in *common sense*. They desperately need it. Many company policies seem to be made in the dark, without considering their effect on customers.

Get a Life

But being right yourself, when the other side is not, doesn't always help you, and there are times when you must recognize this.

I have a designer friend who creates terrific stuffed animals. She was in one of the large discount stores once and saw an unauthorized copy of one of her designs. This kind of thing happens often in her industry: one company takes ideas from another company and then incorporates it into their own designs. This particular case was significantly different. Here it was clear that some other company (not the store) had made a character using a sample which my friend had provided them a year earlier, and for which she had a contract. There was no question about it.

She decided to approach the other company to address the problem. When they refused to offer any explanation and denied that they had taken her design, she felt she had no alternative but to sue them.

In turn, they sued her back, a suit which they had to drop when the facts of the case came out. This is a company that is notorious for stealing people's ideas and not giving them credit.

After two years of going back and forth, they offered my friend $25,000. She knew she was in the right, and she knew they had made over one million dollars in profit from the character based on her design. Twenty-five thousand dollars was an insult.

But the company had enough money to stall, causing her to spend more and more money on legal fees. In the end, being right just didn't matter anymore. She had to decide where her Comfort Zone was and how to settle the situation.

She decided that she just wanted it out of her life. She didn't want to deal with these people any more; it was more important than being right or getting more money out of them. She settled for around $35,000 plus legal fees.

You may think, what a shame, she was entitled to a lot more money. But for her, the money was not the most important issue. Not that she couldn't use the money—she really needed it. But constantly having to deal with this matter was hurting her life. It was making her angry and affecting her health. Once she realized that she had found a Comfort Zone, she could settle it and then move on.

> *It's critical to make sure you're*
> *renegotiating with the right person.*
> *If not, it will be a great waste of your time.*

Finding the Right Person to Deal With

I have spent many hours, days, and even weeks, renegotiating with someone, only to discover that this person really couldn't make a decision, and wasn't able to get to someone who could. In my home, if anyone calls a company and doesn't get a satisfactory response, we always ask, "Did you speak to a supervisor?"

When I ran my own company and a customer spoke to me, the customer received whatever he or she wanted. This is often the case: the higher up you go in an organization, the easier it is to renegotiate any issue and get what you want.

People usually don't like you to go over their heads, but sometimes when you've exhausted every possibility with one individual, you have to either give up or go up. I prefer to go up. It takes tenacity, but you need a little tenacity when renegotiating anything.

A lawyer, who was a participant in one of my workshops, told me he had found that when you want to go up the ladder in any organization, it is a good idea to compliment the person you are dealing with. For example, you might say, "You've done a great job, but I feel I need to speak to someone higher up in your organization. Could you please set that up for me?" Then when he passes you up the ladder, he's likely to let his supervisor know that you've been easy and nice to deal with.

I agree 100 percent with this approach. It's much better to have your current contact as your ally rather than your enemy when he introduces you to his superior. Earlier in my career I did not always use this technique on a regular basis, but I do now, and it's really useful.

The Long Ladder to the Top

At one time while I was working for the telecom company, we had a contract with a company that provided us with billing software. The contract was a complete package, including a monthly maintenance fee that was based on the number of customers we billed each month. As it happens, these billing software packages are monstrous, very costly, and usually have lots of bugs in them. I have never heard of one that was bug free.

After two years of trying to make this particular billing system work for us, we decided we had purchased the wrong package. It was not completely the software company's fault, because during the original negotiations our people had incorrectly described some of our needs. Nevertheless, the software company had promised to provide us with new versions and upgrades as they became available to serve our international needs. Eventually it became clear that the company would not, and could not, tell us when they would have any of these upgrades. Consequently, we decided to move to a company that could service us completely. It was time to renegotiate the contract.

It is very difficult to get out of a software contract. These contracts are written to benefit the software company. When I spoke to our contact at the software company, he informed me that he could make the appropriate decision on his company's behalf. We discussed several different ways our two companies could separate. He came up with numerous plans—but they were all based on our company keeping his software.

I made it clear that we had to move to another billing platform. When he said he would not agree to this, I asked to speak to his boss. He told me that his boss would not speak to me and that his decision was final. (I always love it when I hear that someone's decision is final. Then I *know* I'm not speaking to the right person and my current contact's decisions are definitely not final.)

I told him that if his boss really refused to speak with me, I would go to his boss's boss. He said his boss's boss was the president of the company and he certainly wouldn't take my call.

"We'll just have to see," I told him. "But now we're going to stop all payments until I reach someone I can speak to."

He threatened to sue us.

"Go ahead," I said. "That will really get you far."

Then he threatened to ruin our credit. I told him I really didn't care; I wasn't attached to our credit. None of his threats bothered me, and this really frustrated him, which wasn't my intention, but I know companies would rather do almost anything than start litigation.

After a week, I received a call from his accounts receivable manager, asking where our payment was. I explained my conversation with the salesman and told him I wanted to speak to someone with authority. She replied that the salesman was just trying to keep his commission and had no authority to renegotiate this contract. After all, she knew that we were a good customer who had not missed a payment in two and half years. She promised to find the right person for me to talk to.

The next day the salesman's boss called me. I asked him if he had the authority to renegotiate on behalf of the company in this situation and he said yes. We spoke for about an hour, going over all of the issues. He then offered the same ideas as the salesman. I told him that his salesman had made the same offers, which just wouldn't work for us. He said it was the best he could do.

I said, "Then I'll have to speak to the president of the company." He told me the president wasn't interested in getting involved.

"OK," I said, "we'll wait and see."

Another week went by and the accounts receivable manager called me back and asked me how it went with the VP of Sales. I told her that he had basically made the same offers as the salesman, which were not going to work. I also told her I didn't think we were being unreasonable, and I would like to speak to someone else. She said she would look into it, and then called back to say that I should call their in-house attorney.

I knew this was trouble. First of all, she had probably gone to the attorney to ask him who should handle this, and he had told her he would, but that I needed to call him. He was too arrogant to call me. Corporate attorneys always think they're in power if you phone them. I knew it was a waste of time but I made the call anyway.

The attorney said it was their corporate policy to handle these situations in a particular way, and there was nothing anybody could do about it. Their contract was solid. He told me he had reviewed the contract during the original negotiation, and he now felt everything was fine and they had no responsibility in this situation.

Doesn't your heart warm with love when someone tells you, "I'm sorry, Sir or Madame. It is our company policy to ... etc, etc."

I usually tell them, "Well, we have a policy too. Our policy is not to pay vendors who don't fulfill their part of the contract."

I would like to point out that this is not the nicest way to put it, and certainly doesn't show respect. But even I become frustrated sometimes and just *let it out*. I'm not sure it is particularly effective to throw it back in their face. *Be careful not to be cute or flip.* Using humor effectively is one thing; being cute or flip is another. It can work against you, as it has against me many times.

I realized that this attorney was not going to admit anything was wrong with his contract, and so we were at an impasse. I told him he could either sue us or let the president of the company speak to me.

The attorney replied, "The president of the company will not speak to you."

I said, "Who is this guy? The Pope, or Bill Gates?"

He repeated that the president was far too busy to get involved.

A couple of days later the accounts receivable manager called me again. She was a delightful person, but by now she was getting pretty frustrated. I told her what had happened with the attorney, and she told me all these guys were jerks, and she would have me speak to their CFO. After a minute on hold she transferred me to him.

The CFO immediately stated that he could not renegotiate a business relationship. He just didn't know enough about the contracts to get involved—but he really wanted to hear my story.

I told him the story, including the responses from the sales people and the attorney. The CFO was pretty appalled.

I said that the best thing would be for me to speak with the president of the company. The CFO said he would try to set it up.

The next day he called back and told me that the president would be delighted to speak to me that afternoon, and asked if that was a good time for me.

"Absolutely!"

> *Eventually, the Comfort Zone must be*
> *the same for both parties.*

That afternoon I called the president, right on time. I introduced myself and explained the situation, without going into what it had taken for me to get to him. I also never told him about the offers his employees had made and why they didn't work. (Why bother him with details that would just sound like I was complaining?)

He told me that I was absolutely right: their company had promised to provide us with an international supplement to their billing package which they now could not deliver. He asked me how the domestic side of the package was working.

"As good as any," I told him, "but it's much too expensive for us at our current volume without the international package."

He asked if he could make it more acceptable for us by finding an international package that would compliment what we already had.

I told him that I had been advised it was not their policy to give discounts or change any existing contract.

He replied, "Policies are made to be broken."

I expressed my concern that if we made this deal, his sales people and corporate attorney would be angry and might sabotage our service in the future.

He promised me that no-one would do that, and he told me that he felt personally responsible to make this work. Then he asked the big question. "What does your company expect to pay on a monthly basis?"

I mentioned a very low number.

He almost choked. "Is that the best you could do?" he asked in a low voice.

I told him that I couldn't commit to paying more without knowing the cost of the international segment. I also said that I wanted this to be retroactive for the three months I had been dealing with all the people in his company.

He agreed, and promised to have an international billing system for us to look at within one week.

True to his word, he came up with a well-priced international billing solution that was complimentary to his company's domestic solution. We created an amendment to the contract, which I worked out with their attorney, who miraculously became very nice and pleasant to work with.

I had to be persistent, and basically force them to get me to the right renegotiator. Once I did that, we quickly found the Comfort Zone and came to a settlement.

When You Keep Getting, "No, No, and No!"

It has been said that the ability to be a great salesman depends on how many "nos" you can take. The same can be said about renegotiating. You must have both tenacity and creativity to overcome all of the challenges. When the person you are dealing with says "no" to your proposal, the first rule is *never take it personally*. If you feel the "no" is personal, then you may be the wrong person to be representing your side. If it actually *is* personal, then you really *are* the wrong person.

*Behave as if it's personal
and react as if it's business.*

Remember that I said I would make conflicting statements? Here's another one: it doesn't hurt to ask the other party, "Does your response to my proposal have anything to do with me personally?" You will probably be told that it doesn't. But this is the time to be creative and overcome obstacles. Now you can explore different approaches to create the Common Ground.

Begin to think from the other party's perspective. Ask yourself, "Why are they refusing my proposal? Why don't they want to renegotiate?"

The easiest way to get answers is to be open and ask them a few simple questions:

"What are your needs?"

"What part of my proposal is not acceptable?"

"Is there any part of my proposal which is acceptable?"

What you're doing here is creating an opportunity for the other side to open up to you and give you insight into their thinking. Listen closely to what they say, and then use it to create a new proposal that's closer to fulfilling their needs.

Sometimes in these situations I even ask, "What would you propose if you were in my position?" Surprisingly, the answer you receive will often give you an excellent opening to work with.

Every "no" you get is an
opportunity to be creative.

Look Beneath the Surface

A few years ago I was renegotiating a lease on some equipment. Companies that hold the lease for such equipment are usually not the company that originally sold the equipment. For example, you can purchase a Xerox machine from an office supply company, but the lease is with a leasing company like GE Capital. As far as the office supply company is concerned, they've actually sold the equipment to GE Capital, which then leases the equipment to its customers. In this sort of situation, renegotiating a lease can be difficult.

In the case in question, my client's lease was with a company—let's call it Copy Minus—that was both selling the equipment *and* leasing it through their own in-house leasing program. And this lease had to be renegotiated.

Copy Minus had misrepresented the specifications of the equipment when selling it to my client. As a result, my client outgrew the equipment much sooner than was originally promised. The equipment no longer fulfilled their needs, and so they had to purchase additional equipment. My client wanted Copy Minus to replace their original equipment with new equipment.

Copy Minus was not at all willing to do this. They stonewalled me for some time. I kept pursuing the issue because it didn't make sense to me that they wouldn't work with my client.

After much discussion, I finally got Copy Minus to tell me that the salesman who had sold my client the equipment had left the company. Apparently, he had gotten Copy Minus into several deals similar to ours, and now they simply couldn't afford to help us out. I explained that this really wasn't our problem. Here they had a good customer who was willing to buy more equipment, but just needed some relief on their present equipment so it could be sold and replaced with something that actually fit their current needs.

Eventually, Copy Minus acknowledged that they didn't want to lose my client as a customer—this was the Common Ground.

My client owed $15,000 on the lease. The equipment had a market value of about $9,000. I persuaded Copy Minus to take a buy-out of the lease for $10,000. This was the Solution.

My client then sold the equipment, but only got $8,500 for it. They purchased new equipment from Copy Minus, and received a large discount to make up for the loss and the problems they had encountered. This was the Comfort Zone.

In the Settlement, Copy Minus also wanted my client to purchase a service agreement, which they agreed to do. In the end, everyone was happy.

Never be shy about asking very detailed questions about why a company won't renegotiate. The idea is to get them talking as much as possible.

Keep 'Em Talking

The more they talk, the more you'll understand and be able to use. Listen carefully to everything they say. Their Common Ground will come out—just be patient. Keep asking questions. Even if you know the answer to a question, ask it anyway. If you feel they're not coming clean with you, keep asking why they can't do something.

Many times all they will say is, "We just don't want to."

Then ask, "What *do* you want to do?"

You can also explain that their position just doesn't make sense to you and that you don't understand. Ask them, "Can you please help me out, and try to explain your position more clearly, and some of the reasoning behind it?"

When they don't say anything, go back to "Why?"

They may become frustrated with you. That's OK. But now you *must* make your case at this moment; and whatever your case is, put it in question form:

> "Why would you want to lose a customer?"
>
> "Don't you want to have the opportunity to sell more equipment?"
>
> "Don't you think you should take some responsibility for the actions of your salesman?"

Always be encouraging:

> "We can work this out. You just have to be willing to be a little creative with me. If you could say you want to work this out, then we have a Common Ground to work from. We can create a Solution, and a Comfort Zone, from that Common Ground."

Once they agree, you can give them the solution.

Here's another way to approach it. Lay out all the parts of the puzzle, like a mathematical equation to be solved. Let's use my example: You have the original lease, the original equipment, the new equipment, and the new lease. The equipment company also wants to add in the service agreement to make up for their loss. Now you can assign values to each piece of the equation and move on to finding the Comfort Zone.

Then you can tell the other side, "Somehow you need to give us a discount on the past lease, and we will buy out the lease based on that discount. We'll sell the old equipment on our own, for whatever we can get for it, to make up for what we pay you to buy out the lease. Then we'll lease new equipment from you, because now we have the experience to know exactly what we need."

Once you've found the Comfort Zone, getting to the final terms of the Settlement is much easier.

Giving In Is Not a Sign of Weakness

Whether you're negotiating or renegotiating, it's important to learn to be satisfied with the results. If you have honestly and clearly done your best to represent your points, then be satisfied that the results were the best deal you could get. Remember, no technique, angle, or rule works 100 percent of the time. You're not always going to walk away with the most money, or a deal that resolves all of your issues. It just doesn't work that way.

This is a critical point to understand. You can read every book on negotiating, go to seminars and workshops, train yourself to be the best negotiator/renegotiator in the world, and you *still* won't get the best deal every time. Knowing this, you can relax and feel good about each deal that ends up in a settlement.

At the conclusion of any renegotiation, you're the only one who can judge the quality of your own performance. The other party and those you represent (if you're not representing yourself) will be able to judge *their* performances, but not yours. Other people will always *try* to judge you, but remember, you're the only one who can understand your own experience. Who can ever answer all the "what if" questions anyway?

31

That said, if you can be honest with yourself, you will learn from each experience. Other people's comments about your performance may be useful to you in the future. I discovered a long time ago that I'm the toughest judge of my actions, so why should I feel bad about someone else judging me? I always listen and often learn from what I hear.

If you have simply created a Settlement that allows both sides to move on, then you've done your job well. With this attitude, you'll be much better off in your negotiations, renegotiations, and life. Remember though, this only works if you're honest with yourself. The main point here is: only judge yourself to learn from your actions. Once you create a Settlement that everyone has accepted, you've done your job. Don't berate yourself for things you could have or should have done.

> *Always remember the importance to you and your company of "moving on."*

It's How You Play the Game

I was recently in Peru, a country famous for its sterling silver jewelry. I bought several pieces for my wife and daughters, and for a friend's store. I negotiated the price for about an hour with the local teenage girls who were selling the jewelry. Then I went back and renegotiated the price until I got what I thought was the best deal I could.

As a matter of fact, one of the fellows traveling with me thought that I'd gone too far. I want you to know I was very nice to the girls I was dealing with, and we all laughed a lot during the process. We eventually came to a price that was comfortable for them, and I bought all of the pieces.

A few days later, I was speaking with a Peruvian woman, who asked me if I'd bought any native jewelry. I said yes, and I'd had a great time negotiating. She asked me where I'd bought the jewelry and how much of a discount I'd gotten. I told her where, and that my discount was almost 28 percent. She laughed at me, saying if I hadn't gotten at least a 35 percent discount I had paid too much. I felt like an idiot.

But now I know better, and I still feel I got a great deal. I just paid a little too much. In looking at this objectively I shouldn't feel I was weak for paying more, because at the time of the purchase I felt I got a great deal.

In one of my first jobs as a professional renegotiator I was able to achieve an unbelievable settlement. I saved my client $3,000,000. My commission was to receive 5 percent of what I saved them, so I was owed $150,000 for my services. My usual fee is 10 percent, but they had asked me to take this on for 5 percent with no initial fee. I agreed to lower my percentage because this was one of my first renegotiating jobs.

When it came time to pay me, the president of the company asked if I would accept $125,000 rather than the agreed-upon $150,000. Now they were renegotiating with *me!* I asked if they were happy with the outcome. He said they were extremely happy. I asked if they were satisfied with the way I had represented them. Again he said they were extremely happy.

I said, "Then why should I give you an additional discount?" They just *wanted* to pay less.

In the end I agreed to their terms. Almost immediately, I wished I hadn't. It is not like I had so much money I could be cavalier about losing $25,000. They were a profitable company with plenty of money. I started to beat myself up about it.

Now, however, I realize I learned a great deal from that renegotiation: I don't need to discount my services to satisfy my client. I'm not sure the lesson was worth $25,000, but it was worth something. This company did give me two other projects, which I did very well on and made much more than $25,000. Therefore, giving in here was not even a *sign* of weakness, as I received additional business because of my flexibility.

> *Ultimately, moving on to the next project is always more profitable — financially and emotionally — than dwelling on something that is already done.*
>
> *(I can't repeat this point enough!)*

The Settlement

There are as many ways to settle a deal as there are ways to create one. No one result is correct, and no one result is wrong. Often the Settlement of a renegotiation looks terrific from one side, and not that terrific from the other side. Once you know the details and analyze the deal, you'll usually discover that under the specific circumstances, it was the best deal that could be cut at the time.

Look at the thousands of negotiations and renegotiations going on every day—athletes, for example, renegotiate their contracts almost every season. Seeing the results of these renegotiations, sometimes we say to ourselves, "How could they justify paying so much for that guy?" or "How could they let that star slip through their hands and go to another team?" Announcers at the games always seem to be experts on these renegotiations and give you their opinions throughout the season, based on the performance of each athlete.

But the general managers of the teams, who are actually doing the renegotiations, have to take into account many diverse issues that no one else is aware of. It is not a one-dimensional decision for the general managers. They must try to project the player's future performances based on past performance, injuries, personalities within the team, and salaries, all of which have to be balanced against public opinion. And all along they have to keep in mind who is available to replace the player being let go.

It is not a sign of weakness when, at some point, one side or the other must move on. Sometimes a general manager (GM) will get a good deal by getting one player, only to lose a star to another team. There are always many factors that prevent the GM from meeting the needs and demands of a particular athlete. On the other hand, the manager must often grudgingly give in to an athlete's demands because the team's need for this player looms larger than the cost of the demands. In such cases, it's *not* a sign of weakness to give in to some demands so that you can move on to accomplish something else you need.

The Bulls

It's easy to look backwards and judge the results of sports negotiations and renegotiations. There certainly are obvious ones that just didn't work out. Take the Chicago Bulls. After their last NBA Championship, Michael Jordan retired. The general manager then basically dismantled the team rather than building it around Scottie Pippin and the coach, Phil Jackson. The GM let all the players go to other teams, and started from scratch. As I remember it, he kept only one of the starting players, who lasted just one more season.

From the outside, it seemed as if the GM gave himself most of the credit for the team's success during the previous four or five seasons. He figured that if he could find one Michael Jordan and put together one championship team, he could do it again. When the coach and several key players left the Bulls, everyone thought the GM had done a terrible job renegotiating their contracts.

But what if the GM had picked new players, hired a new coach, and created another championship for Chicago? He would have been considered the ultimate genius in basketball. At the time, he no doubt felt he was doing the right thing for the organization. He didn't want to meet the demands of the remaining players, or perhaps the players wanted to move on and made what they *knew* were unreasonable demands. Maybe, since Michael Jordan had left anyway, the GM could have given in to all of their demands and *still* have had losing seasons, or not made the playoffs. We'll never know.

At the time, I remember many people were saying the general manger was weak in his renegotiations. I don't think he was weak at all. I think he had to weigh the costs versus the benefits. In the end, I am not even sure he was wrong. In the eyes of the Chicago fans he was wrong because he didn't continue with a winning team. But who can, or ever has, sustained a winning team for that long? It's an unfair judgment. Would he have been considered weak if he had given in to the demands of the players and coach? *At the time,* everyone would have said "No."

The public wanted to keep the coach and the team intact even without Michael Jordan. But if the Bulls had gone on playing poorly, the public would have said, "This guy didn't have the guts to start over after Michael Jordan retired." Such a judgment would have been ridiculous, unfair, and downright outrageous.

Don't define this type of situation—or allow anyone else to define it—as weakness. This is great negotiating and great renegotiating. *Give and take, ultimately, is how we all settle our differences.* Sometimes we give a little more and sometimes we get a little more. In any negotiation, or renegotiation, you have to create a balance between what you need, what you want, and what you can get. In the final analysis, you have to decide which balance works for you or your organization. This balance is your Comfort Zone for the deal. You won't always get everything you want. Many times you will give in to demands because your real goal is to settle, whether or not the demands outweigh your needs.

Knowing when Not to Get Involved

Before you renegotiate anything, you have to decide whether or not you want to become involved with the particular contract or situation. You may have a contract that's not working for you, but which, for various reasons, is also not worth renegotiating. How do you make that determination?

First, analyze the situation of the contract in question. Ask yourself the following questions:

- Is the original deal costing me so much that I *must* renegotiate? Remember: cost is not just about money; it can also mean time, energy, and reputation.

- Is this deal affecting my ability to service my customers or conduct my business efficiently?

- Did either party, in some way, not fulfill their part according to the original contract?

- Is it worth my time, or the resources of those I represent, to pursue this issue?

- Do I know the parties involved, and do I have a good sense of how they may react to renegotiating this contract? Always be aware of the history.

If you don't answer these questions first, you'll go into the renegotiation blind. But more importantly, only after these initial questions are answered can you determine if the renegotiation is worth pursuing.

> *You can spend a lot of time on an issue*
> *only to discover that*
> *the only possible Comfort Zone*
> *is simply to walk away and live with*
> *what you already have.*

This realization may come at any point during the renegotiation. As you're going back and forth with the other party, you may eventually realize that your goals aren't worth pursuing. If that turns out to be the case, let it go and move on.

Learn to Finesse

When I was with the telecom company, we had a situation with the law firm representing us for our public offering. At the time, our company, USA Global Link, was often in the press for the many unique and creative things we were doing in the industry (including being first to introduce Internet Telephony and Voice Over Internet Protocol, or VOIP, which now is an industry standard). This law firm wanted to help us go public, and since our Chairman already knew one of their lawyers, this lawyer suggested we use their services.

Our Chairman was very clear when he explained that we'd be happy to use them, but we wouldn't pay for their due diligence activities. Law firms often will agree to take you on as a client, but then say that they first have to do due diligence on you for their own satisfaction. This allows them to rack up fees of $25,000 to $50,000 before they even begin your case—fees you're liable for even if the firm subsequently decides not to take you on as a client.

An attorney from the firm said he wanted to come out to our corporate offices and go through all our books and documents to become familiar with us, so his firm could properly represent us. Again our chairman was explicitly clear. They were welcome to come out and we would make all the information available to them, but this was on their dime. We would, however, put them up in a hotel and pay for their food expenses while they were at our offices. They agreed, and three attorneys came for five days to work through all the documents. Then they went back to their offices and created a presentation for their firm. They were very impressed with our operation and agreed to represent us.

The firm's first invoice had a $65,000 charge for their initial report, including their expenses while they were working at our offices. They charged us for the travel costs as well as for the hotel in our town—that we had prepaid. There was another $10,000 charge for work they had done *after* the due diligence.

Instead of fighting with them we just paid the amount we thought we owed, which was the $10,000. Over the months, we paid every bill on time, except for the initial $65,000. When our investment bankers advised us to wait until the IPO market improved, our company and the law firm parted ways.

We still owed the law firm about $30,000. We received a final notice from them and I called them to discuss the situation.

I offered to pay them $10,000. They said they wanted $47,500, which they felt was half of what we owed.

I explained why we did not owe them the $65,000 which was the balance of the initial invoice. They did not accept our position.

I said we had clear documentation that we had never agreed to pay for their initial due diligence. They argued that our position was valid only if they had not taken us on as a client.

I said, "No, that was not the agreement." Unfortunately, the lawyer who initially made the deal was no longer with the firm and would not confirm or deny the deal.

The attorney in their office who handled these situations was totally unreasonable and difficult, to the point of arrogance. He said he didn't care what the offer was from us: he just wanted to be paid in full.

I pointed out that he wasn't listening. After a few more conversations, I just dropped it. I stopped calling him. Of course, he was too arrogant to call me.

I moved on. It wasn't worth it to me to continue trying to renegotiate with someone who refused to listen. The law firm ended up getting nothing and I ended up paying money out to companies who were willing to cooperate.

I had reached my Comfort Zone with this renegotiation: I had had enough of their attorney and I knew that it wasn't going to get me anywhere to pursue it any further. I moved on.

> *The Comfort Zone is not an exact number or specific resolution to any issue. It is a fluid, moving target.*
>
> *The best thing about the Comfort Zone is that you're the one who defines it. No one else can define your Comfort Zone for any given situation.*
>
> *Your Comfort Zone cannot be judged. There is no right or wrong Comfort Zone. But the existence of a Comfort Zone should make it possible to settle in any given situation.*

Taken together, the Common Ground, Plausible Solution, Comfort Zone, and Settlement create the essential framework of successful renegotiation. Each landmark is a stepping-stone towards the next. Some stages can be reached easily, and others may take several weeks to work through.

Every renegotiation is different. What is critical and does not change is how you behave. The point to remember at all times is that *It's not business, it's personal.* We can only move the renegotiation from one milestone to the next if someone takes control of the renegotiation. This point is covered in detail in the next chapter, *The Secret of the Orange Ball.*

Renegotiation Checklist

There are many ways to get to a Settlement. I've created a checklist of ten specific points to help guide you through just about any conceivable renegotiation. Following these points will make it easier to

---

Preparation Points
(before the meetings begin)

1. *Identify the agreement or relationship that potentially needs to be renegotiated.*

2. *Decide if it's worth the time and effort to proceed.*

3. *Identify who's best equipped to do the renegotiating.*

4. *Create an end goal — your Comfort Zone — and be flexible with it.*

5. *Understand the history of the parties involved.*

---

know who is holding the Orange Ball. It will also help get control of the Orange Ball and get it back if you lose it. (In chapter three, *Hit the Refresh Button*, you'll learn specific, practical techniques for keeping and regaining the Orange Ball.) Whether you're renegotiating a contract, lease, or even a personal commitment, it's a good idea to think ahead of time about how this checklist applies to your situation.

The Checklist is in two sections—preparation for the first meeting, and action items that usually come up after the renegotiation process has begun.

Every renegotiation doesn't necessarily follow this exact sequence. Accordingly, you may complete some of these checkpoints at different times during a renegotiation, and not necessarily in the same order as below:

Action Points
(after the process has begun)

6. **Listen to the other side's perspective and see where it matches or doesn't match the reality of your position.**

7. **After hearing their position, create a plan to get to a Common Ground.**

8. **Ask the other side what they see as a Plausible Solution.**

9. **If you can't accept their Solution, begin to present yours.**

10. **Work with the other side to create a Solution, and the common Comfort Zone will emerge. From there, the Settlement is usually simple.**

The best way to elaborate on this checklist is to provide an example of the ten checkpoints in an actual renegotiation.

I renegotiated a contract which USA Global Link had signed with a very large cable company. The contract was for telecom and IP cable all over the world, and had been signed by our previous CEO/ President. We committed to pay $8 million for the cable from New York to London with a $650,000 deposit, and we committed another $6 million for the Pacific Rim portion with a deposit of $350,000. In total, we had given the cable company one million dollars in deposit. In addition, we had agreed to pay a monthly maintenance fee of $20,000.

The cable company then switched on the service from New York to London, but the Pacific Rim portion, from Seattle to Japan and then on to Indonesia, was not yet ready.

---

1. Identify the agreement or relationship to renegotiate.

Here was the problem: About a year into the contract, it became clear to all of us at USA Global Link that the cable contract was not going to work for us.

We decided to abandon our plan to put cable worldwide; instead, we would lease cable from other companies at one-third the price. There was so much worldwide bandwidth available that leasing was more economical than owning our own cable. Another important factor was that our company had taken a new direction. We were getting out of telecom and had a new plan for a global internet site, Global On Line (GOL)—an international internet meta-hub portal, one site to service the whole world. (This was prior to AOL and Yahoo going global.)

Our contract relationship with the cable company was ripe for renegotiation.

---

2. Decide if it's worth the time and effort to proceed.

USA Global Link's Chairman and I felt it was in our best interest to renegotiate the contract even though it was with a very powerful, very wealthy cable company. They were threatening to sue us if we didn't pay the maintenance fee, and begin paying the $150,000 per month lease on the Atlantic cable.

It was *definitely* worth our time and trouble to get out of this contract. I also had in mind that we should be entitled to get back all, or at least part, of our deposit because we had not actually used any of the bandwidth for which we signed up. At this point, we didn't even have an operational international switch in New York, that could connect to the London switch.

For all of these reasons, to my mind the contract was a joke, and was well worth the time and effort to renegotiate.

---

3. Identify who's best equipped to do the renegotiating.

It was decided that I should do the renegotiating. I had not been involved in the initial negotiation, but I understood our position and all of the parameters of the contract.

4. Create an end goal — your Comfort Zone ...

... and be flexible with it.

The Chairman asked what I thought we should ask for in the renegotiations. I told him we should go for two things: to be let out of the contract, and get back our million-dollar deposit. He agreed. We would reach our Comfort Zone if we got out of the contract with no debt on our books, and got the deposit back. Knowing the reputation of this company, it was a long shot to get back any of the deposit, but we decided to push for it anyway.

5. Understand the history of the parties involved.

I called the cable company and the first person I spoke to was the Executive VP of Sales. He didn't think he was the one his company would want to renegotiate this contract. He said he would find out who that person was, and have them get back to me.

This is a critical point. Never tell your story to the first person you speak with. *Be sure that whoever you end up telling your story to is the person put in power by the company to discuss the issues with you.* This may take several calls, and you may have to go through several people before you find out who the right person is. And many times he or she won't even call you back; they'll wait for you to call so they can feel in control of the Orange Ball. (This never matters to me: I always call back.) *Controlling the Orange Ball doesn't start until you're talking to the right person.*

After a week or two, I called the VP of Sales and he said—as they often do—"Oh, weren't you called back? I was sure they were going to call you. I'll put you through to the correct person right now."

In this case, it was the in-house attorney. (In my experience, when a company has its attorney renegotiating with you, it means they're nervous and want their legal side protected. But attorneys are generally not good negotiators or renegotiators, as we will discuss in a later chapter.)

The attorney wasn't there, so I left him a voice mail stating who I was and the nature of my call. About a week later, I called the attorney again to open the discussion.

6. Listen to the other side's perspective ...

... and see how it matches your side's reality.

The cable company's attorney was adamant that we honor our contract and pay them. I told him that we were changing businesses and didn't need the cable anymore. I listened to all of his reasoning: how they had acted in good faith and given us all this credit, and that it was not their fault that we were changing our business plan.

I replied: "Let me think about what you said and I'll get back to you."

7. After hearing their position, create a plan ...

... to get to a Common Ground.

After listening to their attorney, I didn't think their arguments were very strong. A few days later, I called him back and laid out our argument. I told him that his company knew very well when they sold us the cable that at the time we did not have a working international switch in either New York or London.

The attorney and I decided that we really did have a Common Ground, inasmuch as neither of us wanted this to become a lawsuit. He was actually a very reasonable guy and realized the weakness of their position.

---

8. Ask the other side what they see as a Plausible Solution.

I asked him to make a proposal. I also told him that he had to start returning my calls and not have me continually chasing him. He apologized and agreed. Now I was in full control of the Orange Ball.

He called me back and said they were willing to let us out of the contract if we paid our outstanding three months' maintenance fees of $60,000. I told him this wouldn't work but I thought it was a good start. I asked him to give me a couple of days and I would get back to him.

---

9. If you cannot accept *their* Solution ...

... begin to present *your* side.

When I called him back, I told him that we didn't feel they were entitled to *any* money, and that we also wanted our $1 million deposit back because we'd never used any of the cable. He almost choked. He couldn't believe it. He became angry and asked if I was kidding.

I said that I was absolutely serious. The contract was only a little over a year old and we were not using any of their services. They were a $6 billion company with lots of cash and we felt we were entitled to our money back. We had paid $350,000 in deposits for the Pacific Rim portion, which they couldn't provide yet anyway. The attorney said he had to discuss this issue with his president.

---

10. Work with the other side to create a Solution ...

... and the common Comfort Zone will emerge.

In a few days he called me back and said that they would agree to return $350,000 of our deposit, but not the entire million; they would let us out of the contract, including the past-due maintenance fees; and they wanted $8 million in stock of our new company.

The following week we worked out the details. We received the $350,000 cash and they got some stock in our new venture, which they were excited about. The debt was off our books and we received part of our deposit back, which we deserved.

Writing up the Settlement for this renegotiation was even more difficult because of the "what ifs?" that might occur due to the complexities of the companies involved. This is common in settlements between large companies. *But we did finally settle.*

These ten checkpoints may seem simple or obvious. But they are practical guides to ensure that your renegotiations flow unimpeded, and as you'll see in the next chapter, they can also help you identify who has control of the Orange Ball.

CHAPTER TWO

The Secret of the Orange Ball

The principle of the *Orange Ball* was developed by Dr. Christopher W. Hartnett, retired chairman and founder of USA Global Link and Global On Line (GOL). Chris developed the Orange Ball concept for his own executives who had never been involved in negotiating. It was his method of training people to pay attention to the *process*. When you use this approach, you can always see where you are in a negotiation or renegotiation.

The Orange Ball is a metaphor for control. When you have the Orange Ball, you have control of the process. When you know who is holding the Orange Ball, you can then create a strategy to move the process forward, or a strategy to gain control of the Orange Ball. You cannot direct the renegotiation or move the process in your direction unless you first know who is in control of the Orange Ball. If the process is moving forward without your realizing it, this may well mean that things are not moving in a direction that's in your best interest.

> *The Secret of the Orange Ball lies in knowing who is in control at any given time during the renegotiation process, and knowing how to get the Orange Ball back when you want it.*

The Orange Ball principle helps determine exactly what to do to reach a settlement at any point during the renegotiation. Remember, it's The Common Ground that gives rise to the Solution; then the Comfort Zone produces the Settlement. Controlling the Orange Ball allows you to move the process toward a Common Ground to create a Solution. From here, you can create a Comfort Zone that is satisfactory to both parties.

The following is a summary of Chris Hartnett's description of the Orange Ball. (Note that this entire chapter is applicable to both negotiations and renegotiations.)

FREEMAN'S FIVE PRINCIPLES

2. Secret of the Orange Ball

You must know who is in control of the Orange Ball, and how to get it back, to renegotiate successfully.

Picture five people in a room. One of them is holding an Orange Ball. The Orange Ball represents control. One person is always in control at any given moment in every renegotiation—only one—the person who is holding the Orange Ball.

And here is the crucial point: *Only one person can have the Orange Ball at any given time.* This is true whether there are two or 50 people in the room. At any one time, there is never more than one person in control, and that is whoever is holding the Orange Ball.

The person holding and controlling the Orange Ball may not be the person who is dominating the conversation, and possession of the ball may change many times during a conversation, but only one person can have the Orange Ball at any given moment.

In any renegotiation, to gain ground and win your point—the way you want it—you must have the Orange Ball in your hand. You have to be in complete control of the situation. Period.

Easy, you might say. Not really, because it is necessary to constantly position yourself and maneuver for control of the Orange Ball. When you become accomplished at this, people around you may not even realize you are in complete control.

It's a skill. The goal is to try to be in control of the Orange Ball without being pushy, without making anyone else feel like he, or she, is out of control.

We use the Orange Ball image as a vivid illustration to counter the commonly held view that "being in control is bad."

Control is 100 percent of the game when it comes to effective renegotiation. Anyone who argues against this is dead wrong. Be in control and you will gain ground and get to a settlement in your renegotiation. Lose control—give up the Orange Ball— and you will lose ground and valuable territory in your renegotiation. It's all about control.

There may be times when you will purposely give up the Orange Ball so the other side can win a few points and feel the renegotiation is in their control.

Confused? Don't be. Just remember that the moment you want to gain ground or get a concession, the Orange Ball must be in your hands.

Here is an important tip: always act as if you have the Orange Ball. Assume that you do have it until it becomes obvious that you don't, and then look for the first opportunity to get it back.

Without control, it's impossible to gain ground towards your ultimate goal of asserting and implementing your needs.

If you don't know who has the Orange Ball, it puts you at a clear disadvantage.

As long as you're paying attention, and everything is going the way you want, fine. But once you see that the process is not going in your direction, you immediately need to take back the Orange Ball and regain control of the direction of the renegotiation.

*No one always controls the
Orange Ball all the time.*

Chris says you have to take the Orange Ball to be in control, which is true. However, a lot of people feel guilty about wanting to be in control. Look at it from another angle. If you want things to progress, someone always has to be in control; at any given moment *someone* has to have the Orange Ball. If not, nothing gets done and nothing is settled. Have you ever been in a meeting where no one wanted to make a commitment to do anything, even to move the meeting forward? This is frustrating and a waste of time for everyone. The reality is that having someone in control is good, as long as the control is used fairly.

We've established that someone has to take the Orange Ball, and I agree with Chris that it cannot be shared. You may want to pass it around a bit, but if you want to lead the renegotiation in a particular direction towards a specific result, then *you* are the one who must have the Orange Ball.

It isn't necessary to have the Orange Ball simply for the sake of being in control. If the renegotiation is going in your direction while someone else is in control, that's OK—just make sure you are paying attention.

Passing the Orange Ball

Here's a good example of the Orange Ball principle. This happened when I had a company that imported goods from China. I would hear my assistant, Lisa, dealing with customs brokers, trying to get our goods taken off a ship sooner so that we could get them to our customer on time.

"You may say 'no' to me, but when I get off the phone, my boss is not going to take no for an answer and he is going to get you to say yes."

The brokers on the other end of the line always insisted that their answer would be the same, "No," regardless of who called them.

Lisa would hang up and come over to me. "They said they wouldn't do it, even if you called."

My response always was, "Give me the number."

And she would always respond, "If they do it for you, I will be really angry!"

I explained that her problem was that she never had the Orange Ball when she was speaking to the customs brokers.

When I called and introduced myself to one of them I would immediately hear him say, "I told Lisa I would say no to you, and I am telling you, no." I had to get hold of the Orange Ball immediately.

How? *I took control of the conversation by asking questions.* When I had the Orange Ball I was in control of directing the renegotiation towards my goal.

Whenever you're renegotiating, try to have a sense of what the answers to your questions might be. If you can't do that, then you must be very quick on your feet with a follow-up question that will keep the conversation moving towards *your* goal. (Like playing chess, you have to make your current move based on the next five moves.)

My final question to the customs broker was, "Has anyone ever been able to get past this particular obstacle?"

When she answered, "Yes, in very specific situations," I asked her who decided if goods could leave a ship earlier than originally scheduled. She explained that she made the decision to have the shipping company tag the container when it came off the ship. Once tagged, they would know exactly where the container was and thus it could be available to ship as soon as it cleared customs. But she didn't feel our situation warranted tagging the container.

At this point I passed her the Orange Ball: I asked if she would discuss the types of situations in which she would make such a decision. Now she felt in control, speaking about something familiar, which was under her command. She described all the scenarios that would lead her to make the decision to get a container off the boat first and then expedite it through customs. She also made it clear that she didn't really like doing this because it created extra work for her, including follow-up with the shipping company.

This was my opportunity to take back the Orange Ball, and I chose *her* scenario which best fit *our* situation. She had said that she would expedite a shipment if the goods were already so late that they couldn't be delivered to the customer on time without *her* intervention.

I told the customs broker that if she did not expedite our container, it could take another week. I explained that our goods had been ready in Hong Kong a week earlier, and would therefore have arrived a week ago, but the shipping company bumped us onto the next ship. This particular ship took three days longer than usual to travel from Hong Kong to the West Coast, causing us to be at least a week late already. We were going to be late in our delivery, even *without* her expediting the container.

I explained that the merchandise was part of an expensive advertising campaign, so timing was critical. The stores write the orders to arrive at least two weeks prior to their ad breaking, and we try to give ourselves another week as a cushion. With all the delays we'd be lucky if the container arrived three days prior to the ad. The store's distribution center would then have very little time to break down the container and deliver the merchandise to the individual stores. What's more, some stores charge a rush charge when you're late.

Every ship has a map showing the location of each of its containers. Containers are usually unloaded from the ship within 24 hours. They're then placed at random in the shipyard, where they may be difficult to locate (it can take two or three days). The shipping companies work with the customs brokers for several days to get the containers through customs and ready for pickup.

Often, shipments can be pre-cleared for customs with paperwork alone, and once the container comes off the ship, the goods can immediately be picked up for shipment. But because the containers are not numbered sequentially in the shipyard, the most accessible containers get picked up first. If your container is buried in the shipyard and no one knows exactly where it is, it can take days to get to it even if it has already cleared customs.

In this instance, I wanted the shipping company to find our container and remove it from the ship to the yard first, and then tag it (and its location) so we could access it immediately. It could still take another five days to get it through customs. My main goal was to have access to the container as soon as it cleared.

There was still a chance the container might be pre-cleared. Or, if this didn't happen, it might clear quickly, within a day or two. The issue was: were we going to make delivery to our customer one week late or two weeks late? If we were only one week late we wouldn't lose the order.

Two weeks late would be a disaster. The goods would probably get to the stores four to five days after the ad broke. We would then be forced to pay markdown money to cover the cost of lowering the price to sell out of the merchandise. Our risk came to many thousands of dollars.

I was honest with the customs broker and explained that we were a small company and couldn't afford these potential costs. To save the broker the extra work, I offered to call the shipping company and do all of the follow-up myself.

She appreciated both my offer and our predicament. She agreed to get the container expedited off the ship, mark its location in the shipyard, and get it through customs within twelve hours of the ship's docking. I was in control of the Orange Ball. I thanked her very much, and said that I would contact her within the next few days.

Two days later I called: the ship had docked and our paperwork had cleared. Our container was expedited by our customs broker and would be tagged when it came off the ship; transportation to our customer was already set up, so the container could be picked up immediately.

To thank the customs broker for her hard work, I had our company send her flowers and a box of candy—far less expensive than the cost of shipping the goods late. (Brokers work for independent companies, not the government.)

When Chris and I discussed particular renegotiations, we would always figure out who had the Orange Ball at that point in time. If we determined that we didn't have it, then we would decide whether we wanted the Orange Ball back now, or should let the other side keep it for a while. This analysis is important. You don't want to take control if it is not necessary, *i.e.,* if it could disrupt the flow of the process. This point during the renegotiation is about listening and paying attention. If things are going in your direction, why interfere with the process?

The *Secret* of the Orange Ball in renegotiating is not that you always have to be in control, or that it is important to be in control for control's sake. It is in *knowing* who is in control at all times during the process, and getting the Orange Ball back when you want or need to take control. I cannot make this point too strongly.

---

*Brutal honesty will often get you
control of the Orange Ball.*

Winning Is Getting to Move On

Winning has many definitions in the world of negotiating and re-negotiating. Is the winner the one who pays the least amount of money? Is the winner the one who gets the most money? Can you win without the other side losing? Is money the only gauge of winning? Is winning getting what you want at the expense of the other side? Is winning what it's all about?

The answers are: No, No, Yes, No, No, and No. It all depends on how you define "it."

When the "win-win" concept first came out, we all loved it. It seemed so fair! Over the years, however, I've changed my mind. Don't get me wrong: "win-win" works, and it's a great goal when renegotiating. But like anything else, it is not absolute.

Initially, every renegotiator said, "Well, we'll just create a win-win for everyone."

At the time, I thought to myself, "Win-win? Give me a break. I want to win; I don't care if *you* win or not. It's not my responsibility to make sure *you* win also. It's your responsibility to take care of yourself and if you don't measure up, that's just survival of the fittest." (And by the way, I don't always win, so why should you?)

But I learned that win-win is not a bad thing to achieve in any renegotiation.

Being stuck in a conflict costs companies millions of dollars a year. This is where you want to remember the phrase "Cut your losses and move on."

I don't believe that settling and moving on qualifies as a win-win situation. As I've said, and will continue to point out, not every settlement is fair, or the best conclusion for each party. I don't believe we have to label every transaction we conclude as a "win-win" just to justify an abstract goal.

A landlord who renegotiates a lease with a tenant and gives up revenue is not winning. He may have decided to make the deal for several reasons, but it is not what he really wanted. Some people will argue that the landlord did win because he kept the tenant and got to move on to something else. It's a credible argument, but you can't tell me that the landlord walked away celebrating, feeling as if he'd won.

> When renegotiating, it is more important
> to reach a settlement and move on
> than to worry about who wins.

We all want to win, to get what we want, to achieve our goals. But because winning is not always possible, we should learn to lose graciously. Live to fight another day—or understand that concluding or settling a renegotiation makes it possible to move on, which is neither winning or losing.

But what if winning means keeping your job? Making a living for your family? Doing the best for your company and their bottom line? Scenarios like this put our backs to the wall and tempt us to use the Great Spin to make sure that we win. Would you be willing to lie to win? Would you be willing to cheat to win? Should you have to sacrifice your integrity to win? How far will you go and how far off the mark will you be able to justify your actions? Will your superiors accept losing, ever?

The circumstances going into any renegotiation will color what you will define as a winning scenario. You may tell yourself that it will be OK to lie as long as it doesn't hurt anyone. But you have to define "hurt." Don't get me wrong: we all do it and I'm no saint. I'm just saying, don't fool yourself into thinking that you're within your rights to lie or cheat "a little" to justify winning. This kind of justification is what created the common saying, *It's not personal, it's business.* I believe that our behavior can, and should, reverse this.

There are trade-offs in life, and it's important to know who you are and what you're capable of. I have a friend who is a great businessman. He has been very successful and has become extremely wealthy. I also think he's a lousy negotiator and renegotiator. He has a very high level of integrity, but he also happens to have very little flexibility; he sees everything in black and white. You can't accomplish a lot when renegotiating if you're not flexible and creative.

A good renegotiator can give the appearance of being flexible without actually giving up one inch.

Flexibility and creativity in your thinking are key to your ability to control the Orange Ball and move the renegotiation forward. Not all of us are flexible, or have the ability to be flexible or creative all the time. I've been in situations in which I behaved very inflexibly or couldn't find any creative angle. The important thing here is to *recognize it.* This is the time to be even more patient than usual. Take a step back and hit the Refresh Button, which we'll discuss in the next chapter.

Recognizing our own limitations and having the desire to overcome them, or at least being able to work around our limitations, are critical to our success. If you recognize these limitations in yourself, don't beat yourself up; we all have strengths and weaknesses. In the case of renegotiating, you might want to consider having someone else represent you. Please understand that recognizing our own weaknesses is a wonderful strength. We'll discuss this at greater length in chapter five, *Call in the Cavalry*.

Let's say that I have a particular point on which I am absolutely not going to budge. In other words, I have no flexibility regarding this point. How I present this is critical. If, right from the start, I *say* that I'm not going to budge, I may hit a brick wall on the other side. I'll get a much better reaction if I just make some light comment on the point, or don't even mention it until it actually comes up in the discussions. There's no use pushing your agenda, or a point that you feel is important, until you are sure it's an issue with the other side. When it does become an issue, I often just say, "Let's leave that until the end."

The key is never to seem to be inflexible. Otherwise you get nowhere with the other side. Please note that I never use the word *opponent* when discussing the other side. I don't like to think of them that way. I don't want either party to regard themselves or one another as opponents. If this happens, the entire process of the renegotiation changes color.

Give Your Ego the Day Off

One night I was flipping TV channels and settled on *Good Morning, Miami*, a sitcom about a radio station. I came in about three-fourths of the way through the program, so if any of you saw this particular episode and I have some of the facts wrong, give me a little license here.

A guy who worked at the radio station—let's call him Mike—was renegotiating his contract. He told the station's owner that he had received an offer from a station in New York, and he was considering moving unless the owner met his demands. He then told his girlfriend, who also worked at the station, about the offer.

She was upset and sad that Mike might be moving. When he and his agent went into the owner's office to settle on the final agreement, Mike got everything he wanted: more money, longer guaranteed contract, and a private bathroom. He signed the contract and came out of the office triumphant. He had controlled the Orange Ball and won the renegotiation. His girlfriend was happy and everything was great.

Right after the deal was done, Mike's agent said goodbye to him and before leaving the office, she congratulated him on "the New York angle" and how well it had worked.

Mike's girlfriend took a step back. "You made that up? You lied and really didn't have an offer from New York?"

Mike told her that it was just a little lie. He had done it for them, so they could have a better life, with more money and stability.

"But you put me through all this anguish," she said. "I was really upset, and you stood there and let me believe that you were going to leave me for a job in New York."

He said that it was over now, it didn't matter.

"You are right about it being over," she said. And broke up with him. Mike told her he was sorry, but she wouldn't listen.

Now he had his contract, but did he really win? He lost his girl-friend, and when word gets around that he lied to get his new contract, he will lose the respect of his co-workers. There is an old saying: be careful what you wish for because you just might get it.

Why did Mike lie? Most likely, he was not confident that his agent could renegotiate the best deal for him, and he had no confidence in his own skills—he doubted that he was really worth what he was asking for. In Mike's mind, he felt that to be in control of the Orange Ball he had to create a situation that would give him an edge. He wasn't renegotiating for himself; he was renegotiating for his ego.

What would have happened if Mike had just been honest? Probably he would have made less money, with a shorter contract, and no private bathroom. In the end though, he would still have his girlfriend and the respect of his colleagues. Instead, he will probably use the Great Spin to convince himself that he won because he got what he wanted. However, he still has to live with himself. *That* is the ultimate test.

> *Lying is always a dangerous game to play.*

Be Honest and Respectful

Being honest is one of the best techniques for holding and regaining the Orange Ball. The question isn't whether or not to be honest; the question is when to let all the facts out. In an earlier story, I didn't tell the attorney from the other side that I was willing to accept anything less than the total refund of our $1,000,000 deposit.

It wasn't that I misled him about wanting the full deposit back: that was the truth. I did want it all back and I thought we deserved it, but in the end I was *willing* to settle for less.

Being honest does not mean that you have to tip your hand. I was in control of the Orange Ball. I was leading the renegotiation toward my goals. Some would argue that this might not have been completely straightforward. Do you remember that in the introduction I said I might make contradictory statements? Well, this is one of them.

It's important to test the waters when renegotiating with anyone. Although I did feel we deserved our complete deposit back, I never thought it was *likely;* but I didn't feel it was wrong to ask for it. In my opinion, this is perfectly honest, straightforward, and in keeping with my integrity. I wouldn't have been embarrassed or felt that I took advantage of anyone even if they *had* given us the entire deposit back.

To keep both your integrity and your control of the Orange Ball, only give out as much information as is needed at any particular time during the renegotiation. If you provide too much information, you could sacrifice your position. If you provide too little, then you won't move the process along as quickly as you could. It's a delicate balance.

Most of the time it's better to be cautious and err on the side of telling too little rather than too much. You can always tell more at a later time, but it's almost impossible to take something back.

Greed Doesn't Pay

A friend of mine owns a nationwide company that takes photos of marathons and graduations. Once, several rolls of film were somehow lost either at the event site or at the lab they were sent to. The lab reimbursed the company for the loss, but the company still wanted the negatives back. The lab said that they obviously didn't have them.

About a month later, a woman (independent of the lab) called the photo company and said she had found the negatives, and asked if they were interested in getting them back. The company indicated that they would like them back, even though they didn't really have any use for them anymore. She agreed to send the negatives if the company would be willing to pay her for returning them. She wouldn't give her name or phone number, so they couldn't call her. Every time the company offered her a specific amount she would agree, and then call back and try to renegotiate the amount.

The president of the photo company eventually realized that the woman was calling on the company's 800 number, and he asked the phone company to trace her number back to her name and address. Then he called the lab and asked them if they knew the woman. They said yes, that she had quit their company about the time they had learned the negatives were missing. The authorities were called, and she was probably prosecuted for theft or fraud.

Let's forget for a moment that she stole the negatives. If, in her negotiations and renegotiations, she had not been so greedy and had agreed to send the negatives back, and been grateful for any reward, she would probably never have been caught.

Too Smart to Be a Liar

When I was around twelve, I lied to my mother about something. She told my father, and when he came home he sat me down and asked me if I had lied.

I decided to come clean and said, "Yes."

"Son, do you realize how many people are in jail for lying and cheating?" he said. "The jails are filled with them. And do you know why they're in jail? Because they're not smart enough to lie and cheat and get away with it."

He told me that there are as many people in jail for lying and cheating as there are liars and cheaters who don't get caught. He asked me if I knew the difference between the ones who get caught and the ones who don't.

I told him I thought it was luck.

He said absolutely not. He told me that the ones who didn't get caught were smarter than the ones who got caught. Plain and simple. He then asked me, since I had just lied, whether I was a smart one or not so smart?

I said I wasn't sure.

He told me that I must not be too smart, because I got caught.

I felt bad. Not only did I get caught lying, I was also being told I wasn't that smart.

My father explained that I was extremely bright, I just wasn't smart enough to be a professional liar and cheater. He said that if

I continued on the path of lying and cheating, I was bound to get caught, so it was in my best interest not to lie and cheat.

My father was one of the most moral, honest people I've ever known, sometimes even to a fault. This story was his way of trying to keep me on the straight and narrow path. The conversation had a big impact on me. I'm not saying I've been perfect since I was twelve years old, but I can say that I have a reputation for dealing with people in an honest and respectful way.

In the end, all a business person has to hang his or her hat on is reputation. Any time you enter into a renegotiation, you bring your reputation with you, whether the individual you're dealing with knows you or not. People get a sense of who you are from their first conversation with you. Once you understand how to present yourself so that the people you're speaking with feel that you are honest and forthright, you'll gain their confidence. That's because *it's not business, it's personal.*

> *The key is: you actually have to be honest and forthright.*

If you start out *acting* honest and forthright, and end up being dishonest and deceitful, you'll create a difficult time for yourself. There are people who become known for this pattern. They begin the relationship in an honest way, but soon show their true colors. Once they get a reputation for behaving this way, it's difficult to change it; it catches up with them. Being honest and forthright shows respect to others, and usually earns respect in return.

Behavior

Our behavior creates our reputation. If we behave well, people will want to deal with us. If we behave badly, they won't.

None of us is perfect. I'm sure you won't believe it, but from time to time, I've behaved badly. I'm not proud of it, but it usually goes like this: first I get tired, then I get frustrated, and then I behave in a way that I later regret.

The worst thing about behaving badly is that *it doesn't help you.* Screaming at someone doesn't encourage them to move in your direction. Most people either close down or become defensive when they're attacked. And if they take the offensive, you're still no better off. The key is to try to remain calm, whatever may be going on. Always be alert not to push the other person's buttons.

No matter what we may do, or how we may behave, sooner or later we have to deal with people who think they can behave any way they want, and who will use anger and deceit as a way to control the Orange Ball. This is why I keep saying to *behave* as if it's personal, and *react* as if it's business.

The Path of No Return

At one point I was renegotiating all of the accounts payable for USA Global Link. We had decided it was time to liquidate some of our under-utilized assets. We had several pieces of real estate, which we decided to sell in groups. One group—three office buildings and two standard lots—had a total value of around $1 million dollars. We had put about $1,250,000 into these properties. We lived in a small town, and at the time neither commercial nor non-commercial real estate markets were doing well. Nothing was really selling.

There was a fellow in town—let's call him Mr. Cheatem—who had gone to the school of "No Down-Payment Real Estate." He had a reputation for buying extremely cheaply, and on his terms. I knew him personally: not well, but he wasn't a stranger. The guy came off as being very nice.

Mr. Cheatem called me and we set up a meeting at the largest property. He said he'd be interested in purchasing the package if the price was right. He understood that we needed help, and he was willing to help us by purchasing the property. He was taking control of the Orange Ball—being a great guy who was doing us a favor.

I knew his reputation and I was skeptical. Ninety-nine percent of the time people don't buy things or make deals that cost them money, just as a favor to someone else. They always want something in return. This guy was not one bit interested in us. He saw an opportunity to steal the property and disguised it as altruism.

I had also heard from Mr. Lowball, a representative of a group of local businessmen who were interested in purchasing this same package. I had heard of Mr. Lowball: he was a straight shooter and would not set me up. He told me on the phone that his group was only interested in the package if they could steal it.

I said that I appreciated his honesty and asked him what price he would consider a "steal." He told me that if he could get the package for $250,000, his group would be interested. I didn't think that would work, but I appreciated his offer and his honesty. I told him that if they could come in with a better offer I would consider taking it back to the Chairman of the company.

Now I had only one offer, which put me back to negotiating with Mr. Cheatem, who wanted to do me a "favor." He came to me with an offer of $350,000. I took that back to the Chairman and we agreed to let it go for $450,000. We settled with Mr. Cheatem at $400,000.

At the closing he asked, "What guarantee do I have that some creditor won't come back and sue me, saying that I paid under-market value, and force me to give it back?" He wanted a portion of the money set aside for this purpose. We decided to put aside $15,000, and if he did not get sued within 12 months we would get that money back.

Cheatem countered that he wanted to keep all the money, pay us no interest, and, if he didn't get sued, he would pay us the $15,000 a year later. Our Chairman knew this guy was up to something. Even our lawyer knew he was sneaky and not honest. But in the end, Mr. Cheatem's argument was deemed legitimate under the circumstances.

The chairman got on the phone with him and said, "Listen, you have a reputation for ripping people off, and I don't want to be put in that position. I want you to make a commitment to me that you won't pull anything funny in order not to pay us."

Mr. Cheatem assured the Chairman that he had changed, and was just protecting himself.

A year went by, and Mr. Cheatem had not been sued. I called him for the money and he said that he had counter claims against us. I thought to myself, "Here we go."

The collection of the $15,000 was important to us for two reasons. First of all, it's the principle of the matter. Secondly, the company wanted the money to go to a good friend who had previously served the company and had become extremely ill. He was one of our lawyers in town and had warned us about doing business with Mr. Cheatem.

Mr. Cheatem came up with $157,000 worth of claims for things he said we hadn't cleaned up. According to the contract, anything left in the building would either be subject to a daily charge or became his property.

I said he had to be kidding. Our records showed that the three buildings had been cleaned out and that we paid more than $1000 for the labor. The little that was left in the buildings was his to sell. I'd even gone through the buildings *with* him, and he had said everything was fine. This whole thing was a ruse to avoid paying us the $15,000.

I then spoke to his secretary who told me, on the side, that Mr. Cheatem always did this so he could claim the loss on his income taxes. What a racket! He had promised that he wouldn't pull this stuff and here he was, pulling it. I told him he had to pay and he'd better not try to cheat us.

Think about how Cheatem behaved. He drew us in, all the time controlling the Orange Ball. He behaved reasonably and congenially in order to get his price. At the closing he decided to change the deal, on what appeared to be a legitimate concern, and held back some money. But instead of allowing us to put the money in an escrow account, he said that he would just pay it under the conditions of the note.

Now he was refusing to pay, under a false premise. You can imagine how angry we were. We decided to sue him. Unfortunately, he couldn't find a lawyer in town who would represent him, and none

73

of the lawyers working for us would deal with him. Finally a good friend of mine, a lawyer who had represented him on another matter, spoke to him and let him know that I was generally very reasonable. Cheatem offered us half.

I lost my temper and sent him e-mails saying that his terrible reputation had not changed. He responded that he'd never speak to me again because I'd called him names. Again, he was taking control of the Orange Ball, using any tactic not to pay us and not to deal with us. I called mutual friends and spoke with Mr. Cheatem's partner, but unfortunately he hadn't been a partner on our deal. This went on for months.

Finally, we told Mr. Cheatem about a mutual friend who had cancer and needed money to keep his family afloat during the months of chemotherapy and radiation. "If you pay the $15,000 directly to him," we told him, "we'll waive our claim."

He said this was fine, but he would pay only $6,000 because we had hurt his feelings. This guy wouldn't even behave in a human way when the money was going to someone else who truly needed it. We would have held out, but our friend was getting sicker and sicker, so we settled.

> *Choose carefully whom you decide to get involved with in both your personal and professional lives.*

Mr. Cheatem has since left town and probably won't return. Word has gotten around that he hasn't changed; he knows his reputation is terrible. (We recently heard from him. He said he was starting a spa overseas and, because he felt bad about his last transaction with us, he would like to give us an opportunity to invest at a very special rate of return. Can you believe this guy thinks we'd ever do business with him again?)

You have to be careful about being led down a path of no return with someone who intends to take advantage of you. But there's only so much you can do to protect yourself. If you smell a situation like this, back off. Life's too short.

Not Being Attached

It's difficult to avoid becoming attached to the outcome of your renegotiation. I don't want to give you the impression that this is an easy task. (I'll speak more about attachment in the following chapters.)

When I was young and got very upset about something, my mother would say, "Let it go; no one's going to care in 100 years." At this point in my life, I can say that no one is going to care in only 20 years—if that long. I think back on all the things I've been attached to in my life, especially in raising my children or with my wife, my family, or friends, the arguments we had which make no sense at all now—do such things really matter? The same concept applies when you are renegotiating *anything*.

The best—and I mean the *very* best—renegotiators are never attached to the outcome of a deal. Or, if they are, they certainly hide it well.

The process works best when you're dealing with people who are pleasant and who treat you well, people who are honest and upfront when you approach them to renegotiate. They will let you know what they expect; they're fine if you don't want to agree, but they may not move from their position. And if they lose the deal, they're fine with that. If you learn to behave this way, then when people deal with you, their approach will likely reflect yours. It works that way.

Remember checkpoint two of the Negotiation Checklist? *Decide if it is worth the time and effort to proceed.* This is when you unveil to yourself those aspects of the relationship you're attached to, and figure out if you'll be able to hang on to these points and still create a Settlement. You have to decide ahead of time how far you're willing to go.

> *The less attached to settling you seem,*
> *the better the deal you will create*
> *for yourself or your client.*

Being attached and appearing to be attached are two very different things. You can *seem* unattached to a particular point, but you must decide in advance if you're willing to give it up if you're called on it.

You shouldn't have to make decisions on the spot. You can put off the decision for a later date. Be patient; you shouldn't act impulsively.

Depending on the situation, seeming to be unattached, or even opposite, can work in your favor. But be careful—it may backfire if you play it too strongly, or if your real position becomes too obvious. For strategic reasons, you may assume a *posture* of attachment to something that actually doesn't mean that much to you, just so that when you do give it up, the other side sees you're able to let go of things. Just don't get fancy. It's always better to keep things simple.

Keep Sight of the Real Goal

When I was representing a particular company to renegotiate their accounts payables, I found it was easy to be completely unattached. I told the companies to whom money was owed that there was a limited number of dollars to spread around. Take something now or nothing later; it didn't matter to me. The companies who were stubborn and thought I was kidding ended up with nothing; those who believed me received some money. The whole time, I was just honest and unattached; there's something very freeing about that.

One of the best people I ever renegotiated with was Bill Zimmerman. He owned West Coast Liquidators, the buying arm for his Pick 'n' Save chain, which had about 50 stores all over Southern California. He knew his business and his customers quite well. Mr. Zimmerman was the king of buying closeouts.

When I was with Coffee Imports he would call me once a month to see if we had anything we wanted to close out. Now and then we had something to offer him. I knew he would always give me the lowest price, and he knew I had to find out the bottom value for that particular item. When I sent him the samples of the products I had for sale he would call within a couple of days and give me his offer.

I would always say the same thing, "You've got to be kidding. I know they're worth more than that."

"It doesn't matter," he would reply. "This is what I'm willing to pay. I know at this price I can sell it to my customer." We would argue, but his price was his price. I would then go out and see if I could sell the item for more to someone else. Mr. Zimmerman's deal was this: his price might be low but once he agreed on a price, he bought every piece available and he paid on time.

I would always ask him, "Don't you ever just want something that you can't get at your price, something you are willing to pay a little more for, just to get it?"

He told me that he had a policy never to be attached to any item. Once in a while he would get suckered into buying something for more than he thought it was worth (though it was still a great deal) because he liked the item so much. Inevitably, he would get stuck with it, or have to lower the price to his customer in order to move the item. He would lose his profit in this situation, so buying the product hadn't been worthwhile.

Many times people fear that if they don't take the deal as it is offered, they'll lose the opportunity, even if it isn't right for them or costs more than they want to pay or can afford. They think, "I might lose an opportunity if I don't take this deal." But the laws of not being attached say, "So what?"

I asked Mr. Zimmerman, "Do you have the attitude that every item has a top price to pay, and you'll never go over it? And if so, then don't you lose out on purchasing many products?"

"Yes," he said, "but that's not the point." He was serving his customers with product that he could deliver at a certain price, and he had to make a profit at that price. For him, being attached meant buying the wrong product or paying too much for it, in which case it wouldn't sell and he couldn't make his profit. That would defeat the whole point of being in business in the first place.

He assured me that you never lose opportunities when you want to purchase the right products at the right price. Being patient and unattached always pays off in the long run. Pick 'n' Save stores always had customers and they always had plenty of merchandise.

After he retired, we remained good friends and saw each other a couple of times a year. Again and again, I would see him negotiate and renegotiate for all sorts of things, including real estate, products, and items he just wanted for his house. I saw him make deals and walk away from deals. Once I saw him walk away from an item that he really liked.

I asked, "Why don't you spend a little more and get it? You can afford it."

"That's not the point," he replied. "I'm never attached to anything so much that I would pay any price just to have it."

Everything you purchase has a value to you. Don't ever do more, or pay more, for something than the value you would put on it. If you do, the item will always make you feel bad, and you'll wish you hadn't made the deal.

Listen to the masters; their wisdom is invaluable.

I loved Mr. Zimmerman. His advice was sometimes harsh, but always wise and correct. And I can tell you this: Mr. Zimmerman *always* had control of the Orange Ball. He has since passed away, and I miss him a great deal. I think of him often and the lessons he taught me.

Depending on the deal, being less attached is usually easier when you're negotiating than when you're renegotiating. If the deal doesn't go through, most of the time you've lost nothing. You're back where you started. On the other hand, it's much more crucial to reach a solution and settlement when you're *re*-negotiating, because the existing relationship between the two parties has to change in order for you to move on. This is an important distinction. (Of course, I am speaking in generalities.)

In any given situation you want to seem unattached to any particular outcome, whether or not you really care. *Never let on to anyone that you absolutely must have a particular outcome.* Once you do, you'll lose control of the Orange Ball and you'll end up following someone else's direction.

Good Cop/Bad Cop

Everyone knows about the Good Cop/Bad Cop technique that is often used for interrogating suspects on TV and in the movies. This technique also works for negotiating and renegotiating. Does it always work? No. It can be a good way to control the Orange Ball, but you need to be careful where you use it.

You can be the good cop and use an associate or your boss as the bad cop who is not directly involved in the renegotiations. Then at any time during the renegotiation process, you can break away and get the viewpoint of the other person, the "bad cop." It's not always necessary to make the decision yourself, and it's especially not necessary to make decisions on the spot. Again, renegotiating is about patience and not being impulsive. Using another person to bounce ideas off of can give you an out. I prefer to renegotiate when I'm not the one who can make the final decision.

I say, "I'd like to think about this and get back to you." Or, "I'd like to run this idea by some colleagues and get their feedback." This is a safer approach and helps you to keep control of the Orange Ball.

I once owned a company called United Call, a call center in Iowa with third-party call centers all over the world. I needed to renegotiate one of our customer contracts. Our call center in India was selling long-distance services for a telecom company. We had been selling their product for three months and developed more than 10,000 new customers for the company.

Now we were ending the program because the telecom company had run out of leads. But they also claimed that many of their new customers were canceling, saying they'd never signed up for the service and were victims of fraudulent sales techniques.

We asked for proof. Our telecom client told us they were reviewing more than 2,000 orders and would get back to us after their research was concluded. When we finally heard back, they said there were only 107 questionable orders, all from November and December. They decided to deduct the cost of these orders from our next check.

My partner for this campaign was livid. We decided to renegotiate the contract so that we would get paid for these orders, and I used the Good Cop/Bad Cop technique. In this case, my partner and I were not play-acting. I actually was the calm one and he was definitely much more angry than I. Although I wasn't pleased and didn't think their position was fair, I also didn't find it useful to get very upset over it. So my partner could more easily play the bad guy, which didn't bother him, and I could be the good guy.

We presented our arguments to the company. Our main point was that they were too late with their claim. We had no recourse to our call center in India because we had already paid them for these orders and had no other outstanding invoices from which to deduct the costs. We did not feel we should be penalized for the telecom company's accounts payable problems.

My partner threatened to stop doing business with them and to notify the other call centers in India that this telecom company played games with their payments. The telecom company certainly did not want that reputation.

To get to a Plausible Solution, we had listened to the 107 calls in question, and although our sales people could have done a better job on the phone, the majority were fine. I felt that our telecom client had a legitimate complaint with about 30 percent of the calls and I requested they pay us for about half of the 107 orders. They accepted this offer.

Cop Cautions

Be careful using the Good Cop/Bad Cop technique because it can backfire. You have to make sure your partner, the other cop, comprehends the goals.

Many times it's best to get the bad cop away from the scene, or off the phone and e-mail, so the good cop can work calmly with the other side. It's a relief to those you're dealing with, and they'll empathize with the kind of person you must answer to.

Like every other situation, maintain the same principles: be honest, behave properly, and treat people respectfully. Playing the bad cop does not give a renegotiator the right to behave poorly. That never works. Being the bad cop just means being less flexible, less willing to compromise as much as the good cop.

BATNA
Best Alternative To a Negotiated Agreement

Academics in the field of professional negotiating have created the term BATNA, which means Best Alternative To a Negotiated Agreement. It's a time-tested way to look at all the issues of any given negotiation and decide whether you want to continue or walk away. In any renegotiation situation, each side will have its BATNA.

You can create your own BATNA by following the first three or four items in the Renegotiation Checklist presented in chapter one. This procedure will begin to develop your position in the renegotiation process, and will help you to take control of the Orange Ball from your first contact with the person renegotiating for the other side.

You must understand the BATNA of both sides. However, even if the BATNA on the other side seems stronger, it doesn't mean that you can't control the Orange Ball. This is an important point.

When reviewing the other party's BATNA, you might even decide to walk away from the renegotiation altogether. This is part of checkpoint two in the Renegotiation Checklist: *Decide if it is worth the time and effort to proceed.*

I should remind you that this checklist is not necessarily sequential. You may get to checkpoint seven, *After hearing their position, create a plan to get to a common ground,* and then go back to checkpoint two and decide that you need to walk away.

You got to know when to hold 'em,
Know when to fold 'em,
Know when to walk away
And know when to run.

These lyrics from a Kenny Roger's song have been used in several books about negotiating. They're equally true when renegotiating.

How many times have I said that everything in life is constantly changing? Changes cause you to take another look at a deal or relationship that previously seemed perfect, or at least acceptable. Now, however, you want to re-open the conversation and renegotiate to find a better solution and/or settlement.

Even if you feel that you need to walk away from the renegotiation, *leave the door open to come back and open up discussions at another time.* The BATNA for both parties will change over time. Either party might decide at a later date to re-open the discussion in order to renegotiate the situation. I've done this several times after losing control of the Orange Ball.

In this situation I tell the other party, "Right now, I don't see us creating a plausible solution that will result in a Settlement agreeable to both sides. Let's leave it for another day." This may expose you to a lawsuit if you don't continue to make your payments, but you can always come back later to renegotiate. Lawsuits take time; during that time things may change and you may find a new BATNA that will create an agreeable settlement.

A Sticky Landlord

At one time USA Global Link had space in one of the big telecom buildings in New York, and we had to get out of the lease because we had sold that switch and didn't need the space. But that was not our biggest issue. We had put more than a million dollars into renovations, and we wanted to get back some of that money.

For months the landlord not only refused to let us out of the lease, but was also unwilling to return any of the renovation money. Our argument was that the landlord could now get more rent money for the space, and more quickly, because we had done such a good job renovating it. A new tenant now could just move into the space as is.

The rental market in New York was not great during this period, and the landlord didn't want the headache of re-leasing the space, because he already had other space in the building that he couldn't rent. The landlord's position was that the contract stated all renovations belonged to the building and would not be refundable.

I explained to him that this was only the case with minimal renovations. But the renovations we had made were far beyond those most tenants would ever make.

The landlord agreed to let us out of the lease, but he still refused to refund any of the renovation money.

Finally, I told him that although I felt he was being unreasonable and I didn't see any solution, we were going to walk away from the renegotiation for now. I said that if I could figure out a solution, or if his position changed, we could open up discussions again.

He told me that his position would never change, and that he expected us to pay our rent in the meantime.

I told him that I understood. I knew we were not going to continue paying the rent, and he got the idea, too.

He said that if we didn't pay our rent, he would have to proceed with legal actions. Fortunately, we had just paid the rent so it would be at least two months before he could take any legal action.

This time away from the renegotiation gave me an opportunity to find another solution. I thought that if I could present him with another tenant who was willing to move into the space and pay up front for the renovations we'd made, the landlord might be willing to give us back some of that money.

I called the original real estate broker and discussed the situation with him. He said he knew that our landlord and his partners were the toughest in New York and would not budge. I said I wanted to take the chance, and asked if he could find a tenant. The broker told me that it was a long shot but he would try. He made sure, however, that I understood that even if he found a tenant, there was no guarantee the landlord would refund any of the renovation money. The broker offered to call the landlord and feel him out.

I said, "No, I want to come to him with a completed package." I did not want to give the landlord a "heads-up" on my idea.

It took the broker about a month to find a potential tenant. The space was perfect for this new company. They wanted to rent in that building, they wanted to move quickly, and they hadn't found any other space that was already upgraded to their specifications and ready to occupy right away. Our broker went over the costs of the renovations with the prospective tenant, and they agreed to pay for *all* of our renovations. In their mind, it was cheaper than doing it themselves and saved them months of time.

Now I could go back to the landlord with the package. I called him and first asked if his position had changed. He said no. I told him that I might have a potential tenant. He said that was fine, but he would not allow us to sublease the space. I asked why not.

He told me that he would want to charge the new tenant more money for the space than we were paying, and he felt he could also charge for the renovations and make money on that. He had thought of everything. Also, he was within his rights according to the contract. He clearly had the Orange Ball. I decided to take it back immediately.

I said fine, and if that was his position, then we didn't have a tenant. I told him that he could start legal proceedings and I would keep him tied up in a legal mess for months or years. The space would be frozen and he would be out hundreds of thousands of dollars. In the end, he would be stuck with all of the legal fees and a big waste of time with no guarantee of any money.

He was floored. He said I had always told him that I would act honestly with him. I replied that I was, but if he was going to be so inflexible that he wouldn't consider paying us back any of the money we had invested in his space, and if he was also planning to gouge us to make more money for himself, then I wasn't going to cooperate.

He responded by stating that he was within his rights. I said that he knew very well that the intention of the renovations part of the contract didn't cover the level of renovations we had made. Now I told him to be honest with me.

He relented, but said that he would win in court. I asked him if he was interested in winning in court, or being fair now. I had no problem with him raising the square-foot rate on the space if that was the market value, but I wanted our renovation money returned.

He asked me if we really had a tenant. I told him that we did, but I would not release the name until he agreed to give us back the renovation money. He then asked me to send him a list of all the renovations we had made and the corresponding costs.

I sent the list for his review. He got back to me and said he would agree to *split* the renovation cost with us. Based on his understanding, most tenants spent around $500,000 (half of what we had spent) to renovate a space that size. He felt it was fair to pay us the difference. I agreed, and we made the deal. He got a new tenant and we recovered half our money. This was a sticky renegotiation.

BATNA is a good tool. If you're looking for a more detailed discussion of BATNA and how it is used in negotiations, I recommend chapter two of Steven Cohen's book, *Negotiating Skills for Managers*.

Never Renegotiate with Yourself

In this chapter we've covered several different points on how to recognize who controls the Orange Ball, and how to get it back if you lose control. The concept *never renegotiate with yourself* is critical to your ability to keep the Orange Ball.

Believe it or not, we've all fallen into the trap of renegotiating with ourselves. It happens when we make two consecutive offers, bettering our first offer *prior to letting the other side come in with any counter offer.* By trying to accommodate the other side, we may up our offer before getting an offer back from them.

This is a crucial point to remember when renegotiating. When you are *negotiating*, however, it is not as critical because you want to make an initial deal—but I still don't recommend it.

We said that every renegotiation has a history—the two parties are probably somewhat familiar with each other, often tend to be less flexible, and there may be more emotion involved. It's better to take your time, and take one step at a time.

There are many ways to move the other side when they seem to refuse to counter your offer with an offer of their own. The absolute best method is *silence*, even if it lasts for a couple of days or even weeks. Let them work out in their mind what they want to do.

Patience Pays

In China, one of our many subcontractors was a corrugated company who was to provide all of our cardboard. In the past we'd had many problems with the quality of the corrugated cardboard we were receiving, but this particular company seemed to have the quality we needed. Our contract with them specified the type, size, and weight of the cardboard we expected. And when we received the corrugate, the quality seemed fine.

We packed our goods in a container using the corrugate that they delivered. But when the container arrived in the U.S. and our customer opened it, the corrugate had collapsed and there was damaged merchandise all over the place. We had to purchase new corrugate in the U.S., where it costs at least four times as much as in China, and hire U.S. labor to rebuild the pallets with the new corrugate so the merchandise could be put into the stores.

We took the damaged corrugate to a U.S. corrugate company for testing to see if it met the conditions of the contract and found out it did not. I went back to the corrugate company in China with samples of their cardboard and samples of the U.S. corrugate to show them what we expected versus what we had received. I told them I would not pay for the invoice, which was around $50,000. They claimed that they had delivered exactly what we requested on the contract.

I showed them the U.S. corrugate and told them this was the weight that we expected. They said they had delivered the same weight to us, but the structure of the paper used in China is not the same as that used in the U.S. They could provide that quality if we wanted it, but our cost would increase another 50%, because the only way to get that quality was to import the paper from the U.S.

I told them that we would still not pay for the invoice. We had shown them the quality we wanted and they had agreed, and had never mentioned the issue of paper quality.

They understood, and asked me what I felt would be a fair amount for us to pay them. I offered $10,000. They were very upset, and said that they couldn't accept such a small amount. So I asked them what they thought would be fair.

They wouldn't tell me. Instead, they asked me to come up with an-other number. I told them I wouldn't renegotiate with myself. I said they had to come up with a number they would accept.

Again they refused, saying that they really felt they deserved to be paid for the whole invoice. I told them that not only would they not get paid on this invoice, but they would lose our business.

They didn't seem to care. I said OK, and left.

About a week later they requested a meeting in our factory, and I invited them to come down and speak with us. At that time they stated that if we agreed to continue doing business with them, they would accept $35,000 against the invoice of $50,000.

I said that was too much. It seemed to me they were most likely going to try to get back whatever discount I received by charging me more on future orders. Truthfully, however, only half of the shipment was damaged, at a cost to us of about $30,000. So I explained that our cost for the damage was $30,000, not to mention our reputation with our customer, and I expected them at least to take care of the $30,000. We would pay the remaining $20,000 of the invoice.

They responded by saying that they would accept this arrangement if we promised to do more business with them. I said fine, but from now on they had to be completely honest with us regarding the quality of the corrugate. They agreed, and we renegotiated the contract exactly that way.

Throughout the entire renegotiation, I was careful not to be impatient with them, but I also hadn't given them another figure until they responded with an offer of their own. Even though it took a couple of extra weeks, I had controlled the Orange Ball the entire time.

Knowing who is holding the Orange Ball, and how to get it back, gives you freedom to renegotiate. You'll be able to move the conversation towards your goals and your BATNA, not towards the other party's. This is essential in finding a settlement to any issue. Again, don't be afraid to take control. If you have any hesitation or concern, walk away and take some time to think about your goals and the settlement you are looking for.

Don't underestimate the power of understanding the secret of the Orange Ball.

In the next chapter you'll learn how to keep and regain the Orange Ball (while continuing to treat people with respect).

CHAPTER THREE

Hit the Refresh Button

Now that we understand the Secret of the Orange Ball, let's learn how to keep it, and how to get it back if we lose it. If it is true that *It's not business, it's personal,* then our behavior is critical. Through our behavior, we have the power to affect others either positively or negatively, and the opportunity to preserve our own integrity.

The Refresh Button principle can help you move quickly past thoughts and emotions that will not serve you well during any re-negotiation; such reactions can actually prevent you from reaching your goals. When someone breaks a commitment to us, we naturally feel misled, angry, or hurt. No matter how strong our feelings are—or how logically we can defend them—we must be able to set aside our initial reactions and focus on what we are trying to accomplish.

If we've broken a promise or commitment, it's even more important that we learn to behave with restraint, humility, and respect. The first thing we have to do is *admit to ourselves* that we are breaking our word, before we contact the other party. With this admission in mind, our tendency will be to behave with some humility, instead of a feeling of entitlement, when we create our approach.

FREEMAN'S FIVE PRINCIPLES

3. Hit the Refresh Button

Never over-react or act impulsively —

take a deep breath and listen.

The Refresh Button principle gives you an opportunity to stay in control and keep everyone focused on resolving the real issues. It's difficult, if not impossible, to accomplish anything when you, or any of the parties involved, are angry. How many times have you thought: if only we could start fresh, or get the other side to start fresh, things would go more smoothly. By learning how to hit the Refresh Button, you'll be able to facilitate the other side's ability to hit the Refresh Button as well, and your progress will be less likely to be hindered by anger or negativity.

I must give credit to Dr. Christopher Hartnett for creating the Refresh Button principle and developing with me its integration as a key element in successful renegotiations. Over the years, Chris often pointed out to me what he thought I was doing that made me such an effective renegotiator. Our discussions have helped clarify three basic techniques which have consistently enabled me to hit the Refresh Button.

In the next few pages, I'll discuss each of these techniques in depth, because I know that they will help you stay in control of the Orange Ball or get it back when you need it.

Techniques
for getting control of the Orange Ball

1. **Listen**

2. **Be nice**

3. **Use humor**

and also

Get past the history.

Allow venting: it helps.

Listen to both sides.

Don't renegotiate with yourself.

Be prepared.

Getting Past the History

History, as I've said, is what distinguishes *re*-negotiating from ne-gotiating. Generally, whenever we negotiate we are *creating* a histo-ry. Whenever we enter into a *re*-negotiation, *history already exists.*

In a renegotiation, the history includes anything that's occurred between the parties, anything that relates to the agreement or re-lationship in question. Note that even if you have a relationship with someone that has nothing to do with the situation you need to address, that history still means you are *renegotiating,* not nego-

95

tiating. Because you know the person your approach will be different. The way you behave now is even more critical. There is still a history to deal with.

Some renegotiations arise from breaking commitments or promises that were not the result of an original negotiation in the usual sense—for example, government regulations. Regardless of the nature of the original agreement, however, the fact remains that every renegotiation contains a history.

We know that there is always more than one way to look at the same set of facts. How do all parties in a renegotiation—each with his or her own perspective and set of goals—create a Common Ground that will allow them to find a Plausible Solution, and thereby create a Comfort Zone? The answer may surprise you: *the Common Ground is not necessarily based on the facts.*

At the beginning of a renegotiation, unless you, the renegotiator, have already met everyone on the other side, you won't know whether or not they are even willing to discuss the issues with you. You may often find someone who simply doesn't want to deal with you, or with the issue. How do you and/or your client prepare for this? And finally, how do you get the other party with whom you will be renegotiating to address the issues with you?

There isn't any one technique that will get someone to open up to you every time. But there are several techniques that work nine times out of ten.

In any renegotiation, you must get everyone to hit the Refresh Button. In other words, everyone has to step back, take a breath, and agree to take a fresh look at the situation. This is the beginning of establishing a Common Ground.

Why is it so crucial to hit the Refresh Button? Why is it so effective in clearing the air and putting both sides on a track towards a Common Ground? The next few pages should make clear how this principle works in a variety of situations.

Venting

To begin with, we know it's impossible to move the process forward if either party is angry, upset, or generally out of sorts. Indeed, you may have to use this principle just to get your clients into a position from which they *can* move forward. I've represented companies in which there has been a great deal of anger and finger-pointing within. In situations like this, I sit down with my clients and have them hit the Refresh Button so they can look at things calmly and clearly. Only then is it possible to move forward.

Even though the history (the facts) usually has nothing do with the creation of a solution to the issues at hand, both sides may initially have to discuss that history: how the problem was created, and how they reached this point; why one side, or both, cannot keep its commitments. Discussions like this almost always end up in finger-pointing, but they are not necessarily a waste of time.

Note that the process of venting will frequently be smoother when a third party is doing the renegotiating.

It's vital to get a third party involved if the venting is doing damage to the relationship between the renegotiating parties. We'll discuss this more in chapter five, *Call in the Cavalry*. People almost always need an opportunity to vent: it may be an essential part of disposing of the history. And the end of the venting brings the first opportunity for you to have everyone hit the Refresh Button, which, as I have said, must happen if both sides are to be able to focus on the Solution, and arrive at a Settlement.

Listen, be nice, and use humor. These three techniques are what make the Refresh Button principle work.

Learning to Listen

Listening is an invaluable skill that will help you in both your business and personal life. Listening is a learned skill, but the essence of it is this:

---

*When someone is speaking to you,
don't interrupt, regardless of
the emotional tone of the discussion.*

This is very important. You're automatically showing respect to the speaker when you can listen without interrupting. And when you are listening, *really* listen while the other person is talking; you can't just be thinking of how you're going to respond. Don't fool yourself into thinking that the mere *appearance* of listening is the goal.

As the renegotiator, what do you do? *Listen, and listen, and listen again.* It's interesting to hear both sides. Sometimes the facts are the same, but the perspective is different. Listen to everyone, allow them to vent, and *then forget about the history.* Knowing the history does have its place, but to belabor it or focus on it gets no one anywhere.

Most people are actually telling you two things when they speak. If you're silent and listen closely, you'll hear what the speaker is really trying to communicate, but may be unwilling or unable to come right out and say. Only in your own silence will you be able to hear what people are really trying to tell you. Listening is a very powerful tool.

> *Here is an invaluable secret:*
> *all answers come from silence.*

It is in silence that we will discover what people are trying to tell us. When we speak, we are inevitably communicating two things: 1) the words we're speaking, and 2) what we're saying inside, which, more often than not, is what we're trying to communicate but don't want to speak out.

It's like poker: everyone has a "tell," a little nuance or gesture or change in his voice or speech pattern, which signals his intent. During a renegotiation, you'll find the same mechanism at work in every conversation *if you listen carefully.* The answer to your questions will be in the silence. *Don't underestimate the power of silence.*

Eventually, both sides will finish talking, having exhausted themselves venting. Don't interrupt, and don't argue or disagree; you don't have to agree either. You might say, "I understand, it must have been difficult," or, "I can imagine how you must have felt," or, if you want to be more casual, "What a bummer!" Such statements will help settle the emotions of those who are venting.

Be careful not to sound condescending. What you say at this delicate time could inflame either side, creating further arguments, or worse, increasing their anger to the point that they won't want to deal with you or the situation at all.

During a renegotiation, don't ever take it personally when others speak negatively to you, even if they're virtually attacking you or your client. In this situation, it's not personal. The other side may actually be trying to say, "I'm in trouble here and I need your help to get out of it." The renegotiation itself is a personal matter for both sides, but when someone gets upset, they're taking it too personally. That's when you want to hit your own Refresh Button and just let them finish venting.

Contracts Are History

For example, consider a landlord who has a solid contract even though your client can no longer afford the rent. (Ninety-nine percent of the time, landlords have the edge with contracts that favor their interests.) The landlord naturally wants to focus on the contract, and the fact that theoretically the client must pay according to this agreement. This is "the history."

As long as the landlord hasn't done anything that would cause the tenant not to pay, why should the landlord renegotiate the lease? Why would the landlord let the tenant out of the lease?

With the greatest courtesy, you, as the renegotiator, must explain to the landlord that (for example) your client's current conditions are completely different from the conditions that existed when the lease was signed. At that time, your client's company was doing well, they had plenty of capital, and they were in a growing industry. Now, the company has very little working capital, they're losing money every month, and their whole industry is failing.

At this point the landlord can either focus on the lease, or hit the Refresh Button and decide to give the company some relief until it gets back on its feet. If the landlord is too stubborn and balks, at the very least he probably will lose a tenant. You don't want any deposit back, as in the story in the last chapter—you just need relief in the rent. Your request is reasonable under the circumstances.

On the other hand, the client has to understand that the landlord is entitled to be paid according to the lease. The landlord is doing nothing wrong by expecting to be paid. Tenants almost always try to blame the landlord for charging too much to begin with, or for squeezing the company into an unfair lease. Here the client also needs to hit the Refresh Button and focus on the current situation and what they can afford now.

It doesn't matter whether the client wants to get completely out of the lease or just get some relief. Most landlords will work with a client who is forthright, respectful, and accepts that the landlord is entitled to a fair deal. The numbers must speak for themselves on behalf of the tenant if the landlord is likely to help out. (Later in this chapter, we'll discuss several points to take a good hard look at before you sign any lease.)

Being Nice

"Be nice" doesn't mean acting insipid or flowery, or that you should be a yes-person. It means *be pleasant, straightforward, and forthcoming.* One dictionary definition is "exhibiting courtesy and politeness; of good character and reputation, respectable." Define it in this way, and "being nice" becomes extremely valuable collateral. You can be firm in your position, stern even, but you always have to be nice and put your good side forward.

Everyone has a good side and a dark side. Our dark side shows anger and disrespect and tries to overwhelm and intimidate. Revealing negative emotions can only hinder negotiations and renegotiations. Don't assume that showing your good side means you can't still be tough if necessary.

Most of us try to avoid appearing weak. *But being nice (and being fair) is not a sign of weakness; it is a sign of strength.* Real strength comes from the inside; it is reflected in what we say and do—not the other way around. There is incredible strength in being silent, listening, and knowing when to speak.

When I first moved to Fairfield, Iowa, I began banking with a Mr. Lowenberg, who was president one of the local banks. He was an old-fashioned banker. He believed in people, and he gave them the benefit of the doubt. Often he would agree to a loan on a handshake, do the paper work, and later obtain the loan application and the required financials.

Over the years I obtained several loans through his bank. There were times when I would go in for a loan, and like a father, Mr. Lowenberg would ask me questions and drill me on the necessity of the loan. If he didn't feel it was in my best interest, he would turn me down. The point here is that he was so *nice* about it. He said "no" nicer than anyone else I've ever met. He made very few loans that went bad.

Take the approach of listening, being nice, and using humor in all of your business dealings. *Don't change your personality just because you're doing business.* (Unless, of course, you have an especially hard time being a "people person.")

Common wisdom is that we shouldn't be as "nice" in the business world as we are in our personal life; behaving professionally is supposed to mean being "stronger" and "more serious." I completely disagree. Be true to yourself. If you have to behave one way at home, and another way at work, inevitably at some point you will forget which personality to use in which situation. Whether you know it or admit it—you may end up making life uncomfortable for those you care about most. It's a sign of real strength when you can be yourself in any situation.

I admit that this may be more difficult for women, inasmuch as there is still a double standard in business, and maybe in life. If a woman is too nice, men may think she's flirting or coming on to them. I don't proclaim to be an expert in this area, and I'm not sure what the answer is. When this sort of situation comes up, there's always a chance that the behavior *will* be taken at face value and won't be misinterpreted. Let's hope the day is not far off when all people—women and men—are able to behave naturally in business and be themselves.

> *My best advice is to be direct, but nice and easy, so that the person you are dealing with has the opportunity to respond correctly without becoming defensive.*

Perception is very important. I think of myself as an easygoing guy, but my kids and the people who work with me say that I can be quite intense. *The image you think you're projecting may differ greatly from how you're actually perceived by others.* This is why there's always more than one side to every story.

While you're being nice, don't neglect your own well-being. Enjoy your life, and take care of yourself. I find that being nice to people in the midst of dealing with the stress and frustration that often accompany renegotiating, is so much easier when I'm relaxed and feeling good.

In researching this book, I was interested to learn that reducing stress is one of the main objectives of almost all books on negotiation. When you think about it, it's not surprising that making it easier to get results in your negotiations, or renegotiations, would lead to reduced stress and greater harmony and fulfillment. But obviously, negotiating techniques themselves cannot directly reduce your level of stress in life.

There are numerous approaches to reducing stress, not the least of which is giving yourself a chance to unwind. Many people find that specific practices, including exercise, walking, Tai Chi, meditation, and yoga help even more. I've explored some of these over the years, and the most thoroughly researched system appears to be the Transcendental Meditation™ Program (known as TM), as taught by Maharishi Mahesh Yogi. More than 600 scientific studies in 400 institutions worldwide have validated its effectiveness, regardless of lifestyle, belief, or background, and is particularly easy and enjoyable to practice.

I can personally recommend this particular program based on 35 years of experience as a TM meditator and teacher. The TM technique—certainly more than any conceivable *renegotiating* technique!—really can make your life easier, healthier, happier, and much less stressful. But whether it's TM or simply a daily walk in the park, stress reduction should be a given a high priority in modern life.

Using Humor

You can almost always rely on humor as a simple, disarming way to establish a friendly relationship. Humor has often been a formula for success for me.

A few years ago, as an importer and factory owner in China, I found it difficult to understand how the Chinese handle importing and exporting. They're not difficult people, but they operate by different rules and regulations. Sometimes the rules and regulations of one government department completely contradict those of another, so much so that to comply with one department can mean breaking a regulation in another.

My company had a Chinese business license to create and export bath gift sets. Our factory made these gift sets, which we shipped out in many large containers every week. We also sold stationery gift sets, but they were assembled and shipped directly by our printer, who had *different* export licenses required for this type of goods. On one occasion, our printer got behind on our order and asked if he could send the stationery gift set components to our factory for us to assemble and ship out.

I said, "No problem," since we did have the manpower to assemble them, and it was essential to get the shipment out on time. Both gift sets (bath and stationery) were going to the same customer, so we could combine shipments on the same export license: four containers with the bath sets and four with the stationery sets.

But when we sent the eight containers to customs we were told that we could not ship them. Our factory was only permitted to ship bath gift sets. In China your company must have a business license describing not only the type of business you intend to perform, but if it's manufacturing, specifically what you intend to manufacture. Once you receive your business license—no small feat—you then must also obtain a separate export license *for each shipment* that you ship out of China. Your business license lists the specific products for which you are allowed to apply for an export license.

According to our business license, we were allowed to export gift sets with soap, lotions, sponges, and other bath-related items. The fact that we were trying to ship gift sets containing non bath-related items (stationery) in the same shipment was a breach of the letter of the law. The Chinese customs office informed us that we couldn't ship these containers, so I told my people to ship only the containers with the bath sets, and we would deal with the stationery sets later. Chinese customs would not accept this arrangement and confiscated all eight containers.

I started to panic; it even crossed my mind to go down to customs and pay someone off and be done with it. But it wasn't that easy. For one thing, who would I pay off and how much? For another, it's against the law in the U.S. and in China. We had definitely lost control of the Orange Ball.

The customs officials told my customs broker that they would be glad to ship the containers, but they couldn't because of the manner in which the business license was written. The business license officials said they couldn't change the business license because Chinese customs does not allow mixed shipments (*i.e.,* shipments containing different types of items) on individual export licenses. When the different products weren't already defined in the business license, this was a "Catch 22," and a problem that wouldn't go away.

I had met before with several of the officials from both customs and the business license department, and they were all nice people. I decided simply to go to customs and speak with the head of the department. My translator informed me that Westerners weren't welcome at the customs house; however, I was desperate to ship the containers on time. I couldn't wait any longer and I decided to take my chances. So I drove to the customs offices with my customs broker and my translator.

> *Humor is the most dangerous of*
> *these techniques; use with caution!*

The customs building looked like many other Chinese office buildings—a large 1950's-style structure with a huge open linoleum-floored room. A counter ran like a ledge around three of the walls of the room, serving as a place to fill out the proper forms. It was bustling with people, yet quiet at the same time. All the buildings in China, especially the public ones, are spotless, kept very clean by women who are constantly sweeping and wiping everything.

Companies that need appropriate licenses to get their goods passed for shipment send their brokers to this customs building to meet with customs agents. Every company has its own customs broker, as we did. Customs brokers from all the companies sit around on wooden benches and wait for the customs agents to approve their licenses for shipment. Sometimes these brokers wait all day to get their clearance. I never saw the room with less than 50 people in it.

The offices of the customs officials were on the second floor, which was limited to employees only. But since my translator and I had an appointment with the *head* of customs, we were invited upstairs to wait. For about half an hour we sat on hard, straight-backed wooden chairs in the hallway. When he was finally ready for us, we were invited into his office.

The head of customs was a small, thin man. He was 4' 10" at most and weighed perhaps 89 pounds. He had black hair, a round face, and a great smile. Like other government employees, he wore the standard blue uniform of the time and an official hat with a brass badge. He seemed very nice, though quite formal.

After introductions and a few pleasantries, he began the conversation by telling us he had spent the morning looking at our case. He was very sorry, but there was really nothing he could do.

I turned to my translator and asked him to translate what I was going to say exactly, word-for-word. I told him to ask the customs official to please look directly at me. Then I stood very close to the official, so close that his hat fell off when he looked up at me. Peering down, I said, "You are looking at one very large, very stupid American."

I'm fairly tall and a little overweight; compared to this small Chinese man, I was a great white whale. It took a while for my translator to translate this to the head of customs, so there was an awkward moment as I waited for his reaction.

When he finally got the message, I thought he might have a heart attack laughing. This is how I took back the Orange Ball. Humor put me in control and made the customs official want to help me with my problem.

For years I had seen American businessmen operating in China. When they couldn't get their way, they would yell at the Chinese officials, insulting them and telling them that this would never happen in the U.S. Not surprisingly, when the Chinese were treated in this manner they would often walk away and do nothing to help. The behavior of these businessmen reflects poorly on America. (Believe me, dealing with our own U.S. Customs agents is not necessarily any easier.)

"How could I be so stupid," I said to the official, "to think that all gift sets are the same? How could I be so presumptuous as to mix different items on one export license?" I told him that I felt like an idiot and gave him my deepest apologies. I asked for forgiveness, and said this would never happen again. I was learning how to do business in China.

He was still laughing, along with his deputies and my translator—everyone in the room was smiling. But now he began saying that I shouldn't worry and I shouldn't feel stupid. He agreed that it took time to understand how to do business in China.

> *When humor works, it's often a matter of luck.*

I told him that I was very worried because if I couldn't ship these containers, I would not get paid and I wouldn't be able to pay my 600 workers, half of whom would have to be laid off. Everything that I said was true, and I felt it sincerely. This wasn't about business. It was about my showing him real respect and friendliness. Even though initially he did not want to help me, his mind changed because my behavior showed him I was a human being, as he was, not just a businessman trying to push his way through the Chinese customs rules and regulations. I definitely took back the Orange Ball, and now he wanted to help solve my problem.

This story now turns on one of the most important things any re-negotiator will ever learn: *When to shut up—when to actually be silent.* Silence is part of the technique and skill of listening.

I directed my Chinese translator and the customs agent not to say anything further, unless they were asked a direct question, and in that case to keep their answers short. Then I stopped talking. In the silence, the customs official began to think and talk with his deputies. I knew that he was trying to figure out what rule or regulation would allow him to permit me to ship the containers.

We were silent for at least half an hour while he sat there and thought. Every once in a while he would ask my people a question, or call to one of his colleagues and ask a question. After some time he left the room. Another half an hour went by before he returned to quietly tell me that he understood my predicament, but there was nothing he could do. Then he picked up the phone and dialed the head of the business license department. Together they agreed to allow our containers to go through!

We had to again promise him we would never do this again. And that before we tried to ship something, we would get approval from the appropriate authorities ahead of time. I sincerely thanked the man and agreed to be more careful in the future.

One person's humor can be offensive to another; be careful!

When I left, he said goodbye and started to laugh again. "You could stand to lose a few pounds," he said. I told him that I should probably go on a Chinese diet to lose weight. He laughed and replied that rice was good filler food. Then I told him he could stand to gain a few pounds. He said he was trying. Thanking him again, I left with my translator.

Whenever I renegotiate I bend over backwards to keep my principles—not to say that various expedient possibilities don't come to mind, but I almost always pass. In this Chinese experience I was honest, even brutally honest, in admitting "I was stupid." I was friendly and I used humor to disarm. I was not threatening, and I didn't show any disrespect. This process got the head of customs to hit the Refresh Button and help solve my problem. In the end, I achieved my goals and a Solution was found. *Approach* is vital to success.

Listening to Both Sides

Often, when I call a company I'm about to renegotiate with (let's call them Nowayout, Inc.), I explain that I represent the Iwantout company, which has a contract with them. Then I tell them honestly, "I know very little about the details of the contract."

It may seem odd, but initially I also tell my client that I don't *want* to know the details of their problem because it will interfere with my perspective on the truth. It's important to be aware that there is a history, but knowing the specifics of the history *at this particular time* is neither necessary nor useful.

Rest assured that all the details of the history will come out eventually and you'll have to be aware of them. But even before I learn about the details from my client, I tell the representative of the other party that I'd like to listen to their position on the issue. This lets the other side know I'm not trying to sell them a bill of goods which will make their company appear to be in the wrong. Now they're willing to talk, because they know I'm willing to listen. They have a sense that I'm someone who will be fair with them.

And they're right. Even the fact that they're ready to explain their position means that they're setting up the basis for a Common Ground.

The Common Ground will always lie somewhere within their explanation of the original agreement. For example, they may tell me, "I don't understand why your clients think we should let them out of this contract. We're providing the services required, and they have the money to pay us. Why should we take a loss for them? They'll have to come up with a good reason for us to let them out of this contract." Although they're resisting, they're telling me they're *not entirely opposed* to letting my client out—I just have to give them something to work with.

Now I have to come up with a good reason on Iwantout Corporation's behalf. And it must be honest and straightforward. It must also create ultimate *value* (not always in dollars) for the other party if I expect them to consider it. After listening to both sides, it's the renegotiator's job to explain and sell that value.

The cost to my client to get out of the contract will largely depend on the reason(s) that they need to renegotiate the contract. At this point, I go back to Iwantout and ask them to give me the details of the contract and the relationship from their perspective. If this differs from what the other company told me, I'll challenge my client and give them Nowayout's perspective. Now it usually becomes clear who's spinning the truth, and to what end.

I'll ask my clients, "Why should they let you out?" Together we'll come up with a reason that we believe might be acceptable to the other company.

But I have to be careful. Often my client will want to manufacture or exaggerate the problems they've had with the Nowayout company. Yet even when one side *hasn't* performed part of the deal, they still may not be in breach of contract. This is the point where I must come to terms with my client: what they're willing to pay and accept to get out of the contract or deal. This figure, or arrangement, will change during the course of the renegotiations and will ultimately become their Comfort Zone.

The issues in conflict and the reasons for renegotiating constitute the specific history that you, as the renegotiator, must understand. Remember, however, that focusing on it unduly will usually slow the process down.

The history can be especially significant when the other company has *failed to perform its obligation* to such an extent that it has hurt your client. Then you have a truly major renegotiating point. But even in such a case, don't belabor the point. People don't enjoy admitting they're in the wrong, and it can cause the other party to dig in its heels. You may very well have to forget the history and put it aside in order to move the discussions forward.

Because you've listened to both sides at this stage of your renegotiation, you've strengthened your ability to get the parties to hit the Refresh Button. Most people move slowly and at first don't want to give up something that they may ultimately agree to. Always be patient. The discussion will go back and forth until a Comfort Zone can be created.

A woman called me recently, because she was being sued by a contractor she had hired to do her kitchen. She told me he didn't finish the job and she had to pay someone else to finish it. After some conversations, I told her I'd be happy to call her original contractor. She emphasized that she didn't want to have to hire a lawyer and was hoping I could solve it out of court. I told her not to tell me any of the details and I'd get them from the contractor.

When I called the contractor he was belligerent. He asked if I had a copy of the contract and knew the details of the relationship.

I said I did not, and was hoping I could get those details from him. He said he didn't want to talk to me unless I already knew all of the details.

I said OK, but that in my experience the answer to the problem is not in those details. He said that if I was going to move him from his position, I needed to know the details.

I told him that I was not trying to move him, at which time he interrupted me and said that I was losing my credibility. If he had not interrupted me I would have finished by saying that I was not trying to move him on the first conversation. But he was unwilling to listen to me at all and hung up.

I called back in about fifteen minutes and spoke to his wife, who was much more willing to speak to me. She ranted on for a long time, and I just listened. I could see they were very upset with my client.

When I got off the phone, I called my client and asked her for all the details. Quite frankly, the more I learned, the worse it looked for the contractor.

I called the contractor back, but again he wouldn't really listen. He just said to make an offer and he'd show it to his lawyer.

I told him that in my opinion, after reviewing the details, it didn't look good for him. He told me that I really didn't know what I was talking about and that I should make an offer he could show his attorney, and then he hung up on me. I immediately called my client and told her that she needed to get an attorney and counter-sue him.

> When you're wrong, there's nothing like a good old-fashioned sincere apology to get control of the Orange Ball. Come clean; it will empower you.

Here is a case, I believe, where somehow the contractor has it in is mind that he has a slam dunk case. It is very rarely the situation that your case is a slam dunk. The law, the courts, and the jury have a funny way of looking at things that doesn't necessarily go in your favor.

A Cardinal Rule

Never make your best offer the first time around. This is a pre-eminent rule of negotiating and renegotiating. Your offer should always be reasonable, but not necessarily what you will finally accept. First of all, you have no idea what will be acceptable to the other party. Secondly, you need to leave room to maneuver.

Let's say that your client has a viable reason to get out of a million-dollar contract, and is willing to pay $300,000 to do so. Start with an offer of $200,000 or less. But be careful—there's a fine line between insulting the other side by offering too little, and offering too much, thereby forcing your client to overpay.

After a while you will get a sense of what is fair. Sometimes the best offer you can make still may not be fair. In this case, you just want to be honest with whomever you are making the offer to. You can say, "I know this is a low offer and may not be fair, but it's all we can afford." At other times, you may want so badly to move on and get beyond the renegotiation that you make a higher offer than you normally would. Here, too, it's best to explain why you are making such an offer.

If you've made a low offer, then say to the other party, "I don't want you to be insulted by this offer, but it's a starting point, and it's really what my client thinks they can afford (or, is willing to pay). You'll need to give me a good reason why they should pay more."

Using this million-dollar contract example, let's say that you offer $50,000 *or less*. The other side may scream and carry on, telling you that it's ridiculous and that you have to make them a better offer.

Ninety-nine percent of the time, stick to the following rule: Never, ever give someone a second offer before you receive an offer from them. Never renegotiate with yourself.

In this situation, you may well need to hit *your own* Refresh Button to avoid making an impulsive second offer prior to receiving a counter-offer. Every time I have broken this rule in the past, it has made it harder to achieve my goals.

Just because the other side is upset, you shouldn't say, "Oh, OK, we can go to $60,000." Effectively, this would be renegotiating with yourself. In a situation like this, you want to get them to come back with an offer and get them to justify it—even if they end up saying they want $700,000.

Then it's your turn to say, "Ridiculous!" and carry on a bit. Don't take this personally and don't get upset. Enjoy the process! This is part of negotiating and renegotiating. Whether or not the other party has accepted the reasoning behind your offer, they have told you that there *is* a number which will get your client out of the deal, but $50,000 and $200,000 are not it.

This is another critical moment in the renegotiations: when the other side tells you that you have to come up with a better offer. You've established the Solution; now you need to create the Comfort Zone.

As I've already said (and I can't say it enough): never come back with a higher number than the figure you have already offered *before* receiving a counter-offer.

In fact, I come right out and tell the other side that *they* should come back with a number they can accept, because I'm not going to renegotiate with myself. This usually gets a laugh. Now they know that I know what they're trying to do: get me to keep increasing my offer until I reach a number they will accept. It is a ploy.

Instead, I force them to suggest a number that's reasonable to them. Once they do this, it's just a matter of time before I can arrive at a number both parties will accept. In the end, if my clients think they paid too much and the other company thinks they received too little, and neither is completely sure which side I was representing, then I've done my job well.

Finally, whether you're renegotiating for someone else or for yourself make sure that you end on a friendly note. Some of my best friends are people with whom I have renegotiated. At every step of the renegotiating process, you have to remind all parties to hit the Refresh Button, which in turn will provide you with ample opportunities to listen, be nice, and use humor.

Be Prepared

Your approach to creating Solutions in a renegotiation will vary depending on a number of factors, including the type of contract, the nature of the relationship (whether business or personal), and the personalities involved.

After years of renegotiating experience, I like to play a little game with myself. Immediately after listening to both sides of the issue, I write down my forecast of the Solution and the Settlement of the proposed renegotiation. Then I put it away until the renegotiation is concluded, at which point I take it out and see how close I came to what actually happened.

This reminds me of my first job out of college, as a salesman for Coffee Imports International. While selling may seem to have little to do with renegotiating, believe me, renegotiating takes real sales skill, and a good sales person *has* to be a good renegotiator.

We sold to many small gourmet stores, and my territory was Northern California. This was early 1975, when I was 24 years old. On one of my very first sales calls, I visited a store in Santa Cruz. It was Friday afternoon and this was the last store I would visit that day.

This store had previously bought from our company, so this was not really a cold call. I went in, asked for the owner, and introduced myself as the new salesman for Coffee Imports. He responded that I had a lot of nerve coming in to see him when he still had an outstanding order that hadn't arrived yet, and for which he had already bought advertising.

I told him I was unaware of this order and I apologized for any misunderstanding. He said that until we started delivering on time he would never buy from us again.

Here I was losing a customer and I didn't even know what had gone wrong. Was I innocent? Absolutely not. I should have been prepared. I should have known this customer had an outstanding order that hadn't been shipped. Could I ask this man to hit the Refresh Button and start fresh with me? He clearly wasn't interested in doing this and I couldn't blame him.

I decided to drive back to my office (two hours away), pick up his order, and bring it back the next day before the store opened. I left Santa Cruz and arrived at my office a little after six p.m.; I'd called ahead so the order would be ready for me.

It wasn't a big order (the Santa Cruz store was very small): just four boxes, each containing 24 bags of a cinnamon orange tea. We called this item Smell Me Tea because of its powerful aroma. The smell not withstanding, this tea sold really well, which is why the store owner had run an ad for it.

At seven-thirty the next morning I left my house and arrived at the store in Santa Cruz before it opened. When the owner of the store walked up to the door and saw me sitting there with his order, I thought he was going to cry. He said, "No one gives this kind of service anymore: you have potential, kid." From that point, we became life-long friends.

I gave him his tea and helped him display it. Then I asked if we could look through my company's catalogue together and see if there was anything else he might like to buy. How could he say no? My actions had showed him a great deal of respect. For an hour we went back and forth over items we thought he could sell, and discussed the quantity he should buy. In the end, we agreed and I wrote up the order.

The owner told me that he used to own a big clothing store in southern California and had sold it to retire to Santa Cruz. For my age, he said, I wasn't a bad salesman. But to be a great salesman, I should be able to know in advance what items a store should buy.

He told me about an old Orthodox Jewish man who used to come into his clothing store once every three months to sell him the next season's line. The two men would argue back and forth for hours about what the owner should buy. At the end of an exhausting day he would tell the salesman, "OK, you can write up the order."

Out of his pocket the salesman would pull the order, already filled in with all the quantities exactly as they had agreed. That was a great salesman.

I never got to be that good. But I never again went into a business situation, whether it was a sales call, negotiation, or renegotiation, without having some idea of what the order, Solution, or Settlement should be. I understand that this is in contradiction to "not knowing the details," which we will discuss in the next chapter, but sometimes the details *are* important. You just have to know *which* details.

You may ask: Why go through the sales process if you already know what the customer will accept? This is called "massaging the customer." You want the customer to come to the same conclusion that you have reached. Be prepared and do your homework. Be keenly aware of what you know and what you don't know. This gives you an advantage and affords greater control over the outcome of the relationship.

Be humble — it works.

CHAPTER FOUR

Transcend the Details

Volumes have been written about negotiating, most of them by highly experienced negotiators and academicians. The techniques they suggest teach you how to approach any negotiation, and how to deal with specific situations. Many books and articles focus on getting what you want, and suggest techniques to do just that. Others give you steps to follow to reach the Solution. These same techniques are helpful in *renegotiating,* but they're not always appropriate; sometimes they are surprisingly inadequate.

I applaud most of these books, but I take issue with those which advocate that winning is everything, that the most important thing about a negotiation is to beat down your opponent and make as much money as you can. I don't believe this approach helps anyone in the long term. I think it's short-sighted and part of a larger problem in our society. This is why I talk so much about proper behavior in this book.

I've already pointed out that it's easy to become bogged down in details that really have nothing to do with creating a Solution or getting to a Settlement:

> *The details are about the business;*
> *getting to the Solution*
> *is almost always personal.*

This is critical to remember. For example, an impasse can be created by the attachment of each side to its position—meaning the details. Or, people's egos can be too involved in the belief that they are right and/or that they have been wronged. These are the moments when you have to put aside the details; *Transcend the Details* and go beyond them. It's the only way you can hear what the other side is really saying and be able to address their concerns.

FREEMAN'S FIVE PRINCIPLES
4. Transcend the Details
You must go beyond the details to stay on the Critical Path.

Use your creativity. If you want to take control of the Orange Ball, then you must not get stuck in the minutiae. There are *always, always* reasons other than the details of the contract (or commitment or promise) which are preventing someone from agreeing to move forward. But when you get to an emotional impasse in the renegotiation, no one really cares whether the lease originally ran for 5 or 10 years, or entailed charges of $1 or $3 per square foot. Details like these are unimportant at this point, and if you focus on them you will probably not get anywhere. If you listen carefully, however, the other party will tell you, or at least give you an indication, what they need to move forward.

Most people think that the bone of contention in any renegotiation is the money. In reality, this is not so. And even if the Comfort Zone discussion focuses on the money, *the Solution is rarely about money alone.*

If your approach to renegotiation starts out with the money, and makes it the essential point of the dispute, you'll have a very hard time reaching an equitable Solution. It amazes me that most business people, and most lawyers, fail to understand this.

Business schools usually teach that getting the best deal depends solely on paying the least amount possible. This perspective is shortsighted and naïve, if not downright stupid. Paying the least all too often involves beating people down, really squeezing the other parties, or taking advantage of them.

This practice is "bully negotiation," and sadly many business people and lawyers use this technique. I don't recommend it, because it always creates a bad feeling in the relationship.

> *Details can bog down the process.*

Don't get me wrong—sometimes it's appropriate to work and work a deal until you get the very best for yourself or your client. When I negotiate something for money, of course I always try to get the best price. And yes, it isn't my responsibility to protect the other party. Yet I always back off when I feel that I'm starting to take advantage of someone. I have to trust that the other side knows precisely the amount they can accept.

Keep it Reasonable

I once bought 250,000 plush toys from a factory in Korea. When I first heard what the factory owners were asking, I thought their prices were too high. The owners told me this was the best price they could offer, and they were only taking a 15% markup.

I told them that I had no problem with a 15% markup if their cost figures were accurate. I didn't believe they were actually lying; what I believed was that they hadn't calculated their costs correctly.

I asked them to go through all of the costs with me to verify that they were only making 15%. They agreed, and together we went through every item that went into each stuffed toy: thread, needles, wasted material, stuffing, eyes, labor, etc. I guarantee that we covered everything.

When we totaled up their cost against the price they quoted me, it was closer to a 25% markup. On average, this was almost $0.85 per piece higher than the figure they had originally quoted me. The factory owners were shocked and embarrassed.

Then I realized I could reconfigure the pattern pieces to get about 20% more from the material, which saved another $0.10 per piece, which saved me an additional $200,000. The owners had agreed to discount the stuffed toys by almost $0.95, but now it was obvious that they weren't at all happy. I had a long-term relationship with this factory, and I could tell they felt bad about losing another $200,000. I decided it was in my best interest to give them back $0.20 per piece. They were very appreciative and thanked me profusely.

There should be a way to get what you need *and* have the other party feel good about the Solution you've created, or at least feel satisfied that they haven't been bullied or taken advantage of. This takes time and patience. Leaving money on the table for the other side is a sign of integrity. It's a discipline that insures good long-term relationships.

There is an old acronym, KISS (Keep It Simple, Stupid). It's good to keep this in mind when you're renegotiating anything, even the most complicated deal in the world. Almost every time, the whole issue can be sorted into a few simple points. It's extremely easy to get bogged down and distracted with details, which are just the point-value of the contract or commitment. This is not where the Solution lies. It will probably never come from those details.

Listening and Silence

As we've discussed, the first step in any renegotiation is to listen to both sides of the argument. In most cases you will have to let both sides vent. And vent they will, going into all the details of the relationship because venting is always about the details. And with the details, the finger pointing begins. This is OK; it's actually important to let it happen.

Don't try to find the solution in these initial conversations. You may find some valuable points—there are always a few little nuggets of gold revealed by the venting that can be used towards the Solution—but don't try to solve anything during this period.

What's important is to listen. And listen, and listen some more.

As we discussed in the last chapter, when we listen silently and respectfully, we create a rapport with the other party. Our silence transmits the message that we care to spend the time to listen, and this gives them confidence. Our silence conveys a feeling of acceptance that allows the other party to talk to us without fear of judgment and interruption. Our silence provides some hope that we can find a Solution to all of the issues and create a Settlement that will be acceptable to both parties.

While one party is telling you about its side of the conflict, it's important to communicate your concern for their side. You *should* care about their side. Be real. Be understanding. Don't fake anything; these people have feelings, issues, and concerns. Don't pre-judge the situation for or against either side. Everyone deserves your respect. Show it. This is why I keep saying *it's not business, it's personal.*

Even though you understand that the Solution probably has nothing to do with these issues, if you listen carefully you may very well find an angle upon which both sides would be willing to compromise. Or you may discover a subordinate issue that can be easily resolved or satisfied. Pure gold may be discovered when one side says, "If they would only do such and such, I would be willing to...." There it is. It's not in the details of the contract or deal, not how much money they are willing to pay or settle for, but *it is something that they want.*

Remember: listening is not a noun; it's a verb.

Pay attention to your own behavior. Your behavior can override any issue and help to create a solution. If either party becomes stuck on an issue that you know will not produce a solution, your attitude and actions become paramount. What you do, and how you do it, can help them recognize what's truly important to finding a Solution and creating a Settlement. (We'll talk more about this in chapter five, *Call in the Cavalry.*)

Silence Is Golden

As I've mentioned, my first job was with Coffee Imports International in San Francisco, and I was the salesman for Northern California. Because we were a small company, I reported to both the president and the chairman, the two partners of the company. My responsibilities eventually grew beyond selling in my own territory.

Working directly with the president Bill Volkman, and chairman Sal Bonavito, helped me to move up to National Sales Manager within a few years. As our business grew it became essential for us to find new domestic vendors for selected products for our customers across the country. I was chosen to find the vendors and the product.

We sold bulk coffee to several department stores around the country, including Macy's California, Emporium, Bullocks, and several on the East coast as well. We were buying coffee from a roasting company in Chicago, but we wanted a better quality coffee and better control of our inventory. We decided to look for a Bay Area company that did its own roasting.

In the coffee industry such companies were known as "roasters." Since I already knew all of the roasters in the Bay Area, I was asked to open discussions with those I thought could meet our particular needs. It's important to note that although we were selling coffee to the department stores, its sole purpose was to create an atmosphere conducive to selling our coffee machines and other accessories. Even so, it was critical that our coffee be fresh and very high quality.

On one particular day I was selling coffee accessories, mainly espresso and cappuccino makers, to Peerless Coffee, a small coffee store in Oakland that was also a roaster. The bulk of their business was roasting and selling their coffee to the better restaurants and some of the small coffee shops around the Bay Area. I was quite friendly with the owner, George Vukasin. He was a very honorable man and a pleasure to work with. I asked George if he would be interested in being our vendor for our larger store accounts, and if he could he handle the volume while keeping his high quality standards. He said he was sure he could.

Bill and Sal had already met George at several trade shows but they had never really had a chance to sit down and talk. I arranged for them to come to George's store and speak with him. It was a great initial meeting and we met a few more times to taste coffee and work out quantities. When this part was settled, we decided to go forward and work out the prices. A meeting was set up and we spent the morning going over prices.

Bill and Sal had been partners for some time and had developed a kind of sign language by which they could communicate with each other in the middle of a meeting; they could work out what was best for them without anyone else knowing what they were doing. Bill and Sal kept going back and forth with George on the prices. Bill eventually came up with a number that was just a little bit less than what George was offering. Bill knew that it would be a stretch for George, but he also knew that it was still a fair price. It was essential to get this price to make the program work for Coffee Imports.

At this point there was dead silence in the room. George hadn't responded, and Bill and Sal were silent, waiting for a response. George said it was a difficult number to meet. Bill and Sal said nothing. After some time—maybe only about two minutes, but it seemed like hours to me—I popped up and said, "Can't we just work with George's last number and see how it goes?" George immediately agreed. Bill and Sal reluctantly said OK.

Afterwards, in the parking lot, Sal told me that if I ever wanted to get to be on the first team I had to know when to be silent. He told me that George would have eventually agreed, though reluctantly, to the lower price. This would have allowed us to give our customers ten percent rather than five percent advertising allowance on their coffee purchases. The better price would have enabled us to build a bigger and better program with our customers.

Don't be impulsive.

I realized my mistake. I'd been thinking "Here's an opportunity to close a deal," instead of listening to what was really going on. I wasn't paying attention to the fact that silence was OK. More importantly, the lesson of knowing when to be silent was a powerful learning experience. Silence is a technique that can be used in many situations.

Why Some Lawyers Are Seriously Challenged When Renegotiating

Lawyers love details. They are all about details. Ask any lawyer, "Which is more important, the details of the contract or the emotions and relationships that surround the contract?" They will always choose the details. And they are not wrong. When it comes to litigation, writing a contract, or going into a court of law, details are of primary importance.

Lawyers have a hard time moving away from details to look for other angles to find a Solution. Since lawyers create most contracts in the first place, it's hard for them to think that there might be anything "wrong" with a contract that has to be renegotiated. In my experience, very few lawyers like to listen. I think this is because in order to listen one must be silent.

I don't want you to think that I dislike lawyers, or that they're all terrible renegotiators. That wouldn't be a fair statement, because it really isn't their fault. Lawyers are trained to be *adversaries;* they're not trained to be facilitators. They exist to represent you and not give in to anyone, unless it benefits you. This is why it's so important to have lawyers create the contract for your protection. Unfortunately, this role interferes with their ability to help you get out of a contract or agreement. I've seen lawyers who are so arrogant on behalf of their client, that they refuse to work with the other side at all to help create a Solution.

> *When you're trying to find a Solution to create a Settlement, it's the emotions and relationships of the parties that are most significant.*

Many people don't want to deal with lawyers and feel intimidated when a lawyer calls. For this reason, hiring a lawyer to do your renegotiation can put everyone at a disadvantage. If you have a lawyer, then the other side must have a lawyer. And when you get two lawyers talking to one another, that old cash register starts ringing because they're extra careful about what they say, and they're both being paid by the hour.

At one point, the telecom company I was working for received a bill from one of our providers for two million dollars. We knew it was incorrect. As a matter of fact, it was for calls coming entirely from one country in Latin America. It was obvious that this was a case of fraud, but we had to prove it.

We were an international callback company. We had set up a system whereby our customers could call to and from anywhere in the world at huge discounts. They would dial a number we gave them and it would give them a tone and they would then hang up; there would be no charge because no one picked up on the other side. Our switch would recognize what number was calling and then call it back. When the phone rang our customer would pick it up and get a dial tone, and then call anywhere in the world at a discounted price.

For example if you were in Kenya and wanted to dial the United States, the Kenyan PTT would charge at least $1.00 per minute, while we would charge $0.25 per minute. This was a huge savings for our customer but the PTTs hated us because we were going around their systems. Many PTTs in developing countries tried to make callback illegal.

Some PTTs tried to get back at callback companies by doing what's called "hot polling." Telecom companies pay for all calls that come into their switch, whether or not the calls are answered. But because unanswered calls are relatively short, it only amounts to about 2.5 percent and the companies just build this cost into their prices.

The overseas PTTs would obtain an account with a callback company. Then, during the evening or over a weekend, assuming no one would be monitoring call activity, they would start calling your switch. They could make millions of calls an hour. After eight hours of this, if you didn't catch it, you could build up quite an invoice. This is "hot polling."

This Latin American PTT did just this, resulting in a two million dollar invoice from the international provider that connected us to that country. Obviously, it went through their switch as well and they didn't catch it either.

We suspected there was a conspiracy between the Latin American PTT and the U.S. telecom company. Such arrangements were usually set up by a third party. In this case, it was a calling card company out of Europe. Of course no one from the U.S. telecom company would admit complicity. But in our investigation, we found someone from the calling card company who anonymously told us the truth: all the parties knew what was going on.

The truth didn't matter to the attorney at the U.S. telecom company. We had a contract with them; he expected us to pay and would sue us if we didn't. I told him he was nuts (not a great way to create a good relationship—but I needed to wake him up because he just refused to listen). Finally, I told him if he sued us we would counter sue, prove to the FCC that his company was involved, and request that they lose their FCC license. After a while I told him that it was nonsense for us to speak to one another, and that their company should get some business people to deal with the situation.

I got off the phone with the lawyer and called the president of the telecom company. I told his secretary that our company owed their company a lot of money, and we wouldn't pay them until their president spoke to me. The president immediately got on the phone, and was cold and tough right from the beginning of the conversation. I said that he seemed to have gotten a heads-up on our company and I wanted to know what he'd been told.

After he described what he "knew" about the situation, I asked if he'd be willing to listen to our side of the story. He said yes; he was a great listener and remained silent while I quickly stated the situation from our side.

I couldn't tell how he was going to react. He didn't respond at all and just said he would personally get back to me. I asked him to check out certain facts to see if I was telling the truth.

> *Lawyers have fiduciary responsibilities to their clients, which often prevents them from being objective.*

He called me the next day and admitted that everything I said was true, and he apologized on behalf of his company. I then asked him to give us time to pay back whatever we owed once the disputed invoices were settled. He agreed and assigned someone to the case. We worked out the disputes, along with a payment schedule that was comfortable for both sides. So now you can see why this lawyer was not too enamored of me! (By the way, after the disputed invoices were settled we only owed about half the original amount.)

On the issue regarding the Latin American PTT itself, their lawyer did sue us and we counter-sued, though I finally did convince him that we needed to get some business people involved. The business people told me confidentially that they thought suing us was a ridiculous idea, but by then there was nothing they could do about it. Both companies decided to use an arbitrator from the FCC to help settle the case. After six months of testimony and hearings and sending documents back and forth, the FCC ruled in our favor.

I don't blame lawyers for the way they act. As I said, it's their training and their fiduciary responsibility to represent you and get you what you want. However, I do believe that they come on too strong at times. Here is an amusing tale I always like to tell that expresses this perfectly.

A big-city lawyer went duck hunting in rural Tennessee. His first bird dropped into a farmer's field on the other side of a fence.

As the lawyer began to climb the fence, his friends told him it wasn't proper to go onto someone's property here in the South without permission. The lawyer just said, "Don't worry about it," and climbed on over. Just then the property owner, an elderly farmer, drove up on his tractor and asked him what he was doing.

The litigator responded, "I shot a duck and it fell in this field, and I'm going to retrieve it."

The old farmer replied, "This is my property, and therefore it is my duck."

The indignant lawyer said, "I'm one of the best trial attorneys in the United States and if you don't let me get that duck, I'll sue you and take everything you own."

The old farmer smiled and said, "Apparently, you don't know how we settle small disputes like this in Tennessee. We settle disagreements with the 'Three Kick Rule.'"

The lawyer asked, "What's the Three Kick Rule?"

The farmer replied, "Well, because the dispute occurred on my land, first I kick you three times and then you kick me three times, and so on, until someone gives up."

The attorney thought about the proposed contest and decided that he could easily take the old codger. He agreed to abide by the local custom.

The old farmer slowly climbed down from the tractor and walked up to the attorney. The farmer's first kick with his heavy steel-toed work boot dropped the lawyer to his knees. His second kick had a dramatic effect on the lawyer's digestion. The lawyer was on all fours when the farmer's third kick sent him face-first into a fresh cow pie.

The lawyer summoned every bit of his will, and struggled to his feet. Wiping his face with the arm of his jacket, he said, "OK, now it's my turn."

[I love this part....]

The old farmer smiled and said, "No, I give up. You can have the duck."

I've already said that we do need lawyers. They serve an important purpose and you shouldn't get the idea that I don't respect the profession, because I do. It's not often that I skip having a lawyer read the final Settlement or put the final Settlement in writing. For your own protection, you should do the same. I just don't see lawyers as great negotiators, and certainly not as renegotiators.

There is one company, the Negotiation Skills Company—run by Steve Cohen (the lawyer I mentioned in the BATNA section in chapter two)—which trains lawyers to negotiate. A graduate of Columbia Law School, Steve wrote an excellent book called *Negotiation Skills for Managers*. His contact information is in the back of this book. (Steve is a good guy; tell him I sent you.)

To settle any issue or conflict in a renegotiation environment, you do need to understand the details. But don't get so hooked into them that you lose sight of the real issues and the real goals. Creating a Solution for any problem is about looking at all the issues, both factual and emotional, and finding an approach that will lead you to a settlement. Chapter five, coming up next, explores the seven fundamentals of renegotiating—when you get stuck in any part of your renegotiation, take another look at chapter five. Find out which fundamental(s) you need to review, so you can move the process forward.

Call in the Cavalry

*The most pivotal decision you will make
in the early stages of any renegotiation
is to select the right person
to represent you or your company.*

The best reason to bring in a third party is to *remove any emotion* connected with the history. It immediately gives both sides a better opportunity to find a common ground. It's vital to recognize when your ego or agenda does not serve you or your company. When you first realize that you have something to renegotiate, then identify who is best suited to represent you—spending money on an outside professional may be the best money you ever spend. Most outside consultants will work with only a moderate incentive up front and are paid on their performance, based on what they save you.

This chapter is largely about the human ego. We all have one, and it almost always rears up during a renegotiation. We first have to recognize—and then acknowledge to ourselves—that our ego is an obstacle to accomplishing our goal. It's much easier to recognize an ego problem when it's another person's ego creating the obstacles. However—and I'm not claiming to be a psychologist—it's also much easier to detach one's own ego than someone else's.

> *It's extremely difficult for any of us to identify our own ego as a problem.*

Every participant in a renegotiation has a personal agenda (*i.e.,* ego) when approaching the issues. Whether they acknowledge it or not, all participants want their agenda heard and their goals realized. Everyone wants to control the Orange Ball. I spoke earlier about recognizing attachments. It's our egos that become attached to certain issues, and it's our egos that, in some cases, must learn to let go.

FREEMAN'S FIVE PRINCIPLES

5. Call in the Cavalry

Make sure you have the right person renegotiating at all times. If not, call in the cavalry.

From the moment you decide to go into renegotiation, you must decide who'll represent you. You may decide to represent yourself, which is fine. But, as we've discussed, renegotiating is different from negotiating— renegotiation has history. Even if the history has been good up to now and you have a great relationship with the other party, that doesn't necessarily mean you should represent yourself.

Many business people renegotiate a contract or deal with someone with whom they have a great personal relationship, only to ruin the deal and/or the relationship by trying to represent themselves. I've also seen business people call the other party and say, "Listen, we have some issues with our current contract and I need to address them. Because we're so close, I want someone else to represent me. I'd appreciate it if you would hear him out." This legitimate request is usually well-taken.

You may decide to choose someone else within your organization, or go outside and hire a professional to renegotiate on your behalf. *I highly recommend retaining an outside agent, a professional with years of experience, who has your best interests at heart.* And I highly recommend that you do not use an attorney to renegotiate for you—as soon as the other parties hear that they will be dealing with an attorney, they will usually turn to *their* attorney to handle their side. As we've said, attorneys are trained to be adversaries, which makes it difficult to reach a satisfactory result and maintain a good relationship with the other party.

> *There will be times when you start*
> *the renegotiation process,*
> *only to realize that you're*
> *the wrong person to be involved.*

It might be difficult to admit you're the wrong person, but it's healthy and smart when you do. It's far better to come to this conclusion yourself than hear it from someone in your organization. Once you've seen the other party's reaction to your presentation, you may want to reconsider and bring in a third party. That's perfectly all right. If things are not going smoothly, you can simply say, "It looks like we're not getting anywhere here, so I'm going to bring in someone else to discuss this situation with you."

Throughout this chapter, we'll explore specific reasons for choosing a third party, someone with no personal agenda, to represent you and/or your company. Whether this party is within your organization or not, he or she must be removed from the history. *Your third party renegotiator must not be attached to the reasons or causes for the renegotiation.*

Third-party renegotiators must be able to convey a more objective viewpoint, otherwise, they will inevitably either *be thought of* as adversarial, or actually *become* adversarial. Neither relationship will help you reach your Comfort Zone and accomplish a desired settlement. Because there are at least two sides involved in every renegotiation, there will always be some adversarial positioning by both parties, and it is important, even critical, to eliminate it as much as possible.

Choose someone you trust—someone who will bring you clear information that is not filtered through his or her agenda. Someone who will tell you the truth, even if it's not good news. Someone who is neither afraid nor intimidated by you.

Finger-Pointing

In early conversations about any deal that needs to be renegotiated, there will probably be a little (or perhaps a lot) of finger-pointing. When people are trying to figure out what happened or what went wrong (the history), everyone involved will point a finger at someone, something, or even at themselves. However, identifying the issues is not the same as knowing what went wrong; this is an important distinction.

> *What went wrong*
> *is the reason you're renegotiating.*
> *Identifying the issues is the beginning of*
> *creating the Common Ground.*

The finger-pointing generally begins within your own company or group, even before you've spoken with the other party. Listen carefully to what went wrong within your own organization, because you'll be hearing some of these same points from the other side. It's much better to become familiar with these issues before you meet, so you can be prepared to address them when they arise.

No one, absolutely no one, wants to feel that he's done anything wrong, even if he did. Most people will spin a story about what happened to explain why it's not their fault, and deny that whatever created this particular situation had anything to do with them. Very few people (or companies) own up to their shortcomings or mistakes, even when confronted with documented proof. This is why it's so much better if you can avoid dealing with the history, and still arrive at a comfort zone that's acceptable to you and your company.

I've never been in a renegotiation where the history was *not* discussed. This alone is a very good reason to have a third party represent you. It will be easier for a third party representative to "admit" your mistakes, and, because emotions aren't involved, easier for the other side to recognize and admit their mistakes.

The Flip-Side of Finger-Pointing

It wasn't until I was dealing with telecom companies that never admitted their services were less than perfect, that I learned the importance and value of apologizing. One of the companies (let's call it Lotus Minus) gave us a very inexpensive route to India, but unfortunately it never worked.

Our customers were livid and we routinely had to move them to a more reliable, more expensive service. Even when our customers were able to get through on the less expensive route, the party they were trying to speak to couldn't hear them. We constantly had to give them credit. Whenever it came time to pay our bill to Lotus Minus, we would deduct these discounts from our bill.

Finally, enough was enough. I called Lotus Minus and told them that we wanted to get out of the contract and we would not pay our final bill of $30,000. They were adamant that the problem was with our switch, not their routing. We performed circuit tests with them, which proved their route didn't work, and *still* they said it was our switch. I spent weeks and weeks going back and forth with them, to no avail. In this case, getting out of the contract was not the issue, because it didn't force us to use their services. The real issue was paying them the $30,000.

"Listen," I said finally, "we can keep on going around and around. But we both need to move on and settle this issue. We've taken you out of our switch, which basically dissolves our contract."

They eventually agreed to this, but insisted we pay the $30,000. I told them that we had to give discounts off our customers' bills for poor service, amounting to more than the $30,000 we owed them, but Lotus Minus insisted that we had to pay something.

I offered $1,500 and we settled at $3,000. This was still probably too much, especially if you take into account the value of our good reputation and the time we spent on the problem. From that perspective, we lost money in a big way—this wasn't a fair resolution. But in my mind it was more important to move on.

In the end, I learned that I had been too attached. If another person had been renegotiating for me they could have arrived at a Solution much faster than I did. I spent too much time trying to prove that we were right. I should have hit the Refresh Button and moved to a solution.

The other thing I did wrong was to back them up against a wall so that they felt they had to defend themselves. If you put the other side on the defensive, it takes a *much* longer time to find a solution.

Once renegotiations begin, the process of finger-pointing starts up again—much as it may have done when first discussing the issues within your own group. Now, however, you'll gain a different perspective.

Use the answers to the questions on the next page to help determine who should represent you in the renegotiation.

> *Is it a very emotional situation for one or both parties?*
>
> *Does one of the parties feel misled or abused?*
>
> *Is this purely a financial deal that's only about the money?*
>
> *How attached is your company, or the company you represent, to their own point of view?*
>
> *How much does the other party want this situation to be resolved?*

The international telecom company I was involved with bought two switches from a major international switch manufacturer—one for our Denver office, and one for our New York hub. Switches like these cost well over a million dollars each. We had also ordered another million-dollar switch with international capabilities for New York, but the switch was delivered without the international features. By the time the switch manufacturer was able to deliver the missing components, we had decided to return the switch.

When we first discussed who should do the renegotiation of the contract, our Chief Technical Officer (CTO) wanted to take care of it because he had a relationship with the switch company. Right away, everyone involved in the original purchase started to blame one another for buying the wrong switch.

Those who attended the meeting in Miami were saying that before the purchase, the switch manufacturer had flown our people to their offices in Miami, taken them all out on a boat, gotten them drunk, and offered them "escorts." Some of our people felt this situation contributed to our purchasing the wrong switch.

Our CTO completely denied the Miami events had happened, and the switch manufacturer did, too. At this point, the Chairman decided the CTO would *not* be the best person to head up the renegotiation, and asked me to take it on since I had no relationship with the switch company and had not been involved in the purchase.

When I called the switch company, they said it wasn't their fault we purchased the wrong switch, and vehemently denied the boat incident. I said it really didn't matter. I also pointed out that according to our engineering department the switch company was using our Denver switch as a training unit for their employees and for other customers as well. They didn't deny this, saying it was part of the agreement.

I asked, "Was it in writing?" and "Did we get a discount for it?" They said no to both. I told them we wanted to return both switches, and wanted our $100,000 deposit back. The person I was speaking with, the Executive VP of Sales, almost had a heart attack. But he knew I was right. He tried his best to direct accusations at our CTO and engineering department, but in the end he understood that his company had made the bigger mistake by selling us the wrong switch, and using our installation in Denver for training their employees. We returned the switches and they returned part of the deposit. Receiving part of the deposit back was a big concession for the switch company.

Our chairman had been able to take a step back and look at the renegotiation as objectively as possible. If you can do this, then the finger-pointing won't overshadow your decisions. It is also *crucial* that you don't get involved in the finger-pointing, no matter what your position is in the project or agreement being renegotiated. If you start blaming others, then you become part of the problem and not part of the *solution*.

Nonperformance of a Contract

Anyone would that think that it should be a cut-and-dried case when a company fails to comply with a signed, legally binding contract. In such a situation, what does it matter who does the renegotiation?

First of all, in a seemingly simple instance of nonperformance, a company must *admit* to not performing on the contract. And getting someone to admit they didn't perform is very different from the mere fact of their nonperformance. Who is making the claim that the company did not perform? You? The company may not agree with you.

> *Admitting you were wrong or unsuccessful doesn't mean you have to lose everything in the renegotiation.*

The courts are filled with cases in which one party thinks another party didn't perform on a contract, and so both the parties end up suing each other. One side sues for nonperformance while the other side counter-sues. Lawyers bill thousands of hours on such cases, and they don't care which side they are on.

The situation regarding the problems with Lotus Minus and our telecom route to India was not a case of nonperformance. Believe it or not, in most telecom contracts, the quality of service is not a performance issue! Lotus Minus *did* perform according to the contract; they just didn't perform according to our customers' needs. In our minds this was a much more important issue.

People and companies hate to admit that they haven't performed well. They'll usually create the Great Spin to justify their actions and explain why they're in the right. They'll often try to blame *you* for their nonperformance. And they might have a case. This is why I try not to get too involved in the details!

> *Assigning blame is less important (and less effective) than solving the issues at hand. In cases like these, the real goal is just to move on.*

At one time I was renegotiating with three Chinese brothers who were late delivering our product, for which we owed them $80,000. We had a difficult time renegotiating with them, and although we finally made a deal, our relationship with them was jeopardized. In fact, our relationship was never the same. It would have been better to bring in someone else to renegotiate on our behalf. This might have been tricky, because the Chinese like to deal directly with the principals. But as you will see in a few pages further on, we were way too attached to the situation. I would have to say this situation was a close call.

Defective Dolls

I have also been on the other side of the issue. Many years ago my toy company sold dolls to a book and gift company we'll call "Read 'em and Weep." My kids were good friends with the owner, so I knew him socially. We had received a sizeable order, and I had to work on a very short margin to make it work.

The order arrived in two shipments from China, each container carrying the same four styles of dolls. When the first container arrived, it was naturally stopped by U.S. Customs for inspection. I didn't think anything of it. A few sample dolls were tested for safety. Since my agent had already done this, I was unconcerned.

During testing, the second container arrived four days later and passed right through Customs. I shipped it to my customer and they distributed the dolls to their various warehouses. The order as a whole wasn't late so I didn't mention to the customer that the first container was delayed. I assumed it would be released within our shipping window.

Then Customs notified us that one of the four types of dolls (Tabatha) didn't pass inspection. A button had not been sewn tightly enough, and came off when pulled—a loose button is a very dangerous choking hazard for children. So we had Customs pull the Tabatha dolls and return them to the Chinese factory. The balance of the container was then shipped directly to my customer.

Unfortunately, I now had to tell Read 'em and Weep that they couldn't sell the Tabatha dolls from the second container, which they had already distributed to their warehouses.

Even more unfortunately, I wasn't able to reach my friend, the owner, but had to give the news to his Executive Vice President instead. She was furious and accused me of lying to her. She said I should have told her there was a potential problem regarding some of the dolls before she distributed them to the warehouses. I said I had no idea ahead of time that one of the dolls might not pass inspection.

I explained that such inspections are routine in my business and ninety-nine percent of the time there's no problem.

She said I hadn't fulfilled the contract, and she was going to recommend not paying for the entire shipment. This was ridiculous.

"I'm willing to take back the defective dolls," I told her, "and pay for the freight. I'll also give you an aggravation discount." (She was correct that I didn't completely fulfill the contract.) But her argument was that the dolls were merchandisable only if all four styles could be sold as advertised. I suggested that since the dolls were not being sold as a set, each doll could sell on its own merits.

In the end, I had to give Read 'em and Weep a substantial discount, and we lost money on the order. I had to apologize and admit not that we violated the contract *per se,* but that we didn't deliver the complete order at the quality specifications we had promised.

Even though the owner was my friend, I didn't involve him, because it was more important to keep the friendship than to use it to my advantage. Using a friend in business is a recipe for disaster, because *it really is never just business, it's always personal.* I treated this customer the way I would treat any other.

> *Your reputation should always be*
> *more important than your ego.*

Bringing Down the Emotional Temperature

Using a third party to renegotiate reduces the emotional temperature of the renegotiation. Emotion tends to darken (and deepen) the waters of renegotiation. Rarely will anyone react favorably to an emotional outbreak, so it won't help you to reach your goal. And guilt is a poor tactic for getting what you want. It rarely works, it delays finding a solution, and makes you appear weak.

If you have a history with someone it's hard not be emotionally attached; this is only natural. The question is, can you recognize that you're probably not the best person to renegotiate this particular agreement?

There was a perfect illustration of this on one of *The West Wing's* season finales. The President's daughter had been kidnapped, and he realized that he was far too emotionally involved to negotiate the return of his daughter. So he decided to step down and allow the Speaker of the House (who happened to be next in line because the Vice President had resigned the week before) to take his place. It was the right thing to do and the best approach to a delicate situation. With this action, the kidnappers knew that they would have to deal with a person far less attached to their bargaining chip, the President's daughter.

It's not easy to take yourself out of a situation in which you're emotionally involved. Your emotional attachment draws you in to become *more involved.* Nevertheless, if you can see your way to playing a background role in the process, those representing you can more easily and quickly move the other side to a satisfactory conclusion. A third-party scenario usually works well for both sides.

Finding the Right Person to Renegotiate

When you start to renegotiate with anyone, *make sure you're speaking to the right person.* Many companies have layers of people for you to deal with before you get to one who can make a real decision. You may find yourself spending hours, days, and even weeks with people who can't actually bring the issue to a conclusion.

This filtering process goes on all the time, especially in larger organizations. If you ask the person you're dealing with if he or she *is* the right person, the answer will often be, "Yes, I am." But when push comes to shove, you'll often find that person cannot, or will not, make a decision. This can be very frustrating.

From the outset, I try to make sure I'm dealing with someone who has real authority to make a decision. But here's the catch: at each *level*, you *can* get a decision. Unfortunately, the scope of that decision may be limited to the position of the person you're dealing with. As you go up the ladder, you'll be increasingly more likely to find the person who is able to make a *final* decision in your favor.

When I was a company president and a customer finally reached me—after dealing with the other people in the organization and never really getting satisfaction—I had the authority to give the customer what he or she wanted, if it seemed reasonable. Everyone in the company knew that customers who reached me would receive much more of what they wanted than if someone lower down on the ladder settled the issue. As a result, you'll always hear the same answer when you ask for someone higher up: "You're welcome to speak to my boss, but he'll just tell you the same thing." And almost every time, *this is not true!*

Say Thank You First

In one of my workshops, as mentioned in the introduction, a lawyer recounted a technique he uses to move his request up the ladder. He starts by honestly complimenting the person (call him Mr. Smile) with whom he's currently dealing: "Mr. Smile, you've helped me a great deal and I appreciate all you've done (perhaps being specific about what he particularly appreciated). You've extended yourself as much as you can, and now I'd really like to speak to your supervisor, if you don't mind."

This approach makes it more likely that Mr. Smile, your current contact, will say nice things about you when he introduces you to his supervisor. And it's less likely he'll tell the supervisor you're a pain in the neck.

The attorney also told us that the first thing he tells the supervisor is how great Mr. Smile is and how helpful he has been.

Expressing your appreciation is a powerful technique to help reach the right person.

Chairman of the Board

Some years back, I renegotiated some large contracts with a big telecom company. I was dealing with senior vice presidents and their corporate lawyers, but I wasn't satisfied with their response. I told them I wanted to speak to their boss, the chairman of the company. They said he would never get involved and wouldn't even speak to me. My reaction was, "Oh, really?"

It seemed clear from their response that if I *could* reach the chairman, he would not be too happy with the situation and would probably give me what I wanted. "I'll just call him directly," I said, "and take my chances."

If the chairman sided with his own people, I knew they'd become even more stubborn and make it more difficult to renegotiate. They would also be angry with me for going around them, even though I had told them ahead of time that I was going direct. So I was definitely taking a chance, but it seemed worth the risk.

Fortunately, the chairman took my call. I explained our situation and he said (as they had predicted) that he didn't want to get involved and his people would handle it. I told him I'd been dealing with his people, and the renegotiations were not getting anywhere.

Because this was a very large contract, he listened to what I had to say and eventually agreed with my analysis. He told me he'd take care of it. Within twenty-four hours I received a call from the senior vice president, with the corporate lawyer on the line. They were cold, but stated their resolve to be more flexible and to work with me to create a Solution. After a while they warmed up. I apologized for going over their heads, but I told them they'd left me no choice. We reached a settlement that was both fair and acceptable.

The Other Side Refuses to Discuss the Issues

There are times when emotions run so high that one side flatly refuses to discuss the issues with the other side. This is a clear signal that *you need someone else to represent you!* A good renegotiator is able to help both sides get past their emotions by allowing them to vent and getting them to discuss the real issues, in order to arrive at a Solution and Settlement.

History, or past experience, creates emotion—either positive or negative. It's important to assess the "emotional temperature" prior to opening conversation with the other side. Try to get as much information as you can on this before entering into renegotiation.

Will they be blindsided by your desire to renegotiate, or are they aware of the problems? This information will give you, as the renegotiator, a sense of how open the other party will be to renegotiating the agreement.

Don't be surprised if they don't want to discuss anything. Several clients have told me that when they brought up the subject of renegotiating with the other party, the first reaction was, "If you continue down this path, you'll have to speak to my attorney." That's fine, but as I've pointed out, bringing in attorneys can be messy. What the other party is *really* saying is: "I don't want to discuss this directly with you." They may be willing to discuss the issues openly, but threaten to use an attorney because they feel they have no safe alternative.

> When someone renegotiates on your behalf,
> you actually have more control of the outcome
> than if you're representing yourself.

Often you must give up control in order to achieve your goals and an acceptable settlement. In other words, you may have to give someone else the task of renegotiating, so that you can stay in control—behind the scenes. But please take note: you will *not* necessarily have more control of the outcome if you use an attorney, especially if you use an arbitrator.

Many contracts specify that if there is a breach, or if one party wants to get out, the issue will automatically go to an independent arbitrator. An arbitrator is trained to review documents and listen to both sides. The arbitrator then makes a judgment as to which side should win, and creates a settlement, which is usually binding.

You can appeal such a decision, but it's difficult. Often judges will force a case to arbitration if they feel that a full trial is a waste of time. On the other hand, a professional renegotiator represents *one* side and tries to reach a settlement which *both* sides can agree to.

Unfortunately, there are situations where the other side absolutely will not talk to you. Period. They won't answer your calls or respond to your e-mail. In one such case, my client had to get out of a lease. They had been occupying almost half of a building, but now they had moved out. The landlords were very tough guys, they said, who wouldn't even speak to them.

When I called the landlords, however, they spoke to me without hesitation and they had a completely different story. They were upset because my client had left the building without notification. All my client did was send a letter requesting to be released from the lease, never even mentioning a departure. Now the landlords had a half-empty building, and they had no idea what went wrong. I discovered that what the landlords *really* wanted was a formal apology from their former tenants. In the end, they received the letter of apology and we made a satisfactory deal to get out of the lease.

My client had to give control to me in order to gain control of the situation. Before I was brought in, the client had no control because the landlords would not speak to him. By ceding control to me, my client gained an appropriate influence over the renegotiation.

You Made a Mistake — It Happens

Another appropriate third-party scenario is one in which you've made a mistake, or your company has failed meet a contractual obligation. You must get out of the contract, but it's going to be tough because *you* created the problem.

In this situation, you *must* allow someone else to represent you, and you'll have to make the best of it. By "the best of it," I mean that your ultimate goal is just to move on. The "worst" would be for you to be attached to your point of view. This is one of the times to be humble. Apologize sincerely, and ask the person you're dealing with to try to be reasonable with you. Anyone who's representing you should take this approach.

> *I don't believe there are any mistakes:*
> *only wrong turns.*
> *The bigger the wrong turn, the harder*
> *it will be to get back on the path.*

Let's go back: *be honest and straightforward when approaching the issues.* Whoever represents you should begin by saying, "My clients are well aware that they didn't abide by the original agreement. But they still have to get out of this contract." This will provoke various responses, but if you continually repeat these few sentences like a mantra, eventually the other side will move away from anger and blaming, and begin to renegotiate with you. The goal is to get them to a reasonable position in order to settle. Listening to their side of the issue, and allowing them to vent, will help.

> *Learn from your wrong turns.*

Bad Baskets

At one time, my company had a contract with a Chinese factory to make 50,000 wicker baskets in a given amount of time, in three different styles and colors. We would supply them with special wooden handles being produced in another part of China. The basket factory was very large and we were just getting started with them. Normally, they only took orders from other big companies, and did not like taking small orders or dealing with companies that were not financially stable.

The supplier of the wooden handles never delivered them. The wicker factory waited and waited for the handles, which we kept saying would arrive any day. Once we realized the handle factory wasn't going to deliver, we had to go back to our customer in the U.S. and let them know that we could only deliver the baskets *without* the wooden handle. They accepted the situation, provided that the order arrived on time.

When we returned to the waiting wicker factory, they told us they could only deliver *half* the baskets on time. Fine, we said, and told them to cancel the other half. (We'd found another wicker factory that could make the balance of the order on time.)

The original wicker factory was furious; they had already bought, cut, and dyed the wicker for the full order. They wanted to produce the entire order and insisted it was our fault that they couldn't. We agreed, but we still had to deliver the order on time. After all, the basket was only part of the product and we already had all the rest of the components to fill the total order. We couldn't afford to ship only half.

We told the original wicker factory that we would purchase all of their raw material and deliver it to the other factory, which would then make the rest of the baskets on time. It seemed like a good solution and everyone would come out even.

But the original factory didn't want to release the raw material. They wanted us to pay for it, but they refused to deliver it to the other factory. We went around and around. We apologized and said the whole situation was messy and definitely our fault but, nonetheless, we had to move forward.

They threatened to withhold the first 25,000 pieces if we didn't pay for the balance of the raw materials. They would keep the raw materials for us to make baskets at a future date. This was unacceptable because we did not know when, if ever, we would use these raw materials.

It became a question of will. (Also, I really hate being threatened.) So I said no; I wouldn't pay for anything—neither the finished baskets nor the raw materials.

They told me I would lose half the order, and pointed out that I had told them I couldn't afford that.

I said I would ship half, and just work it out with my customer. I knew that the other factory could produce at least half of the baskets on time so we would complete half of the order. But I was not going to be threatened by anyone. I felt that I'd made a fair offer to the original factory, under the circumstances.

Finally, they agreed. In retrospect, however, I believe that we could have settled much sooner if someone else had represented me. The fact that they were speaking directly with me had made it much more difficult for them to make a deal.

Just Hire a Lawyer

As we've already mentioned, lawyers, by training, are generally not good negotiators or renegotiators. They are trained to be adversaries, so naturally they create an adversarial situation. Lawyers almost always try to make it appear that their side is "right," and rarely, if ever, do they admit that their client had any responsibility in the agreement going wrong.

Also, when a lawyer represents you, the other side may feel intimidated and also turn to a lawyer. Then you have the worst of all situations: two lawyers talking to each other; two lawyers trying to *win*. Lawyers (who you might think shouldn't or wouldn't) often get their own egos involved and—surprise, surprise—can come across as arrogant. This is *deadly* when you're trying to come to an agreement. It's also expensive. You're paying your lawyer on an hourly basis to speak to their lawyer. Before you know it, you've just spent $15,000 and you're no closer to solving the issues, much less to defining a settlement.

I know from experience that when we get in trouble, our first tendency may be to hire a lawyer. It's a business person's knee-jerk reaction. *A lawyer should be the last person you hire. Only after you've exhausted all other attempts at renegotiating a previous agreement or contract should you hire an attorney.*

Before deciding who you want to represent you, think about what kind of relationship, if any, you want to have with the other party *after* the dispute is settled. If you honestly don't care how it ends up, then I suppose you can justify anything as long as you get what you want.

However, I believe it's more important to keep your reputation intact and your integrity high. It's better to leave a relationship on good terms. You never know when you might benefit from the relationship in the future. People move around from company to company and one thing they always take with them is their memory. You don't want to end up dealing with someone you've mishandled in the past. This is reason enough to give everyone you deal with due respect.

If you are going to use a lawyer, be sure your lawyer represents you in the way you want to be represented. Don't be afraid to give very specific instructions on how to handle any given situation—including how you want your lawyer, as *your* representative, to treat people. If you suspect your lawyer isn't listening to you, find another one. There's no shortage of lawyers.

The whole point of hiring someone to represent you is so you can control the progress from the sidelines. If a professional renegotiator or lawyer is unwilling to take advice from you, find someone else.

Many times my clients have given me great advice which they just couldn't execute themselves. The chairman of the telecom company was brilliant in this way. When I could clearly explain to him what the other side was saying, he would then come up with a strategy that I could execute. It made our side that much more powerful.

People are always afraid to tell lawyers what to do. You have to remember whom they work for—you. Be respectful, but discuss strategy with them and be clear about how you want to be represented. They have an obligation to listen and do what the two of you have decided together.

But allow me to repeat, I *do recommend* that you hire an attorney to write up the *final agreement* in (almost) every renegotiation. Attorneys know how to write a deal that protects you. It's their shining attribute.

Don't underestimate the value of lawyers.
Don't overestimate their value, either.

Settling Before to Going to Trial

Different situations can be renegotiated at different times during the process of reaching a settlement. You might think that once your lawyers are involved, and you're in the middle of a lawsuit and everyone is preparing to go to court, that you must continue down this path. Not so. Lawyers frequently settle a situation prior to trial; it happens all the time.

What if the lawyers can't settle and there seems to be no other solution? *Understand: in the eyes of the law, once you have a lawyer and the other side has a lawyer, the lawyers are in control.* Your lawyer may only speak to their lawyer, and vice versa. Neither lawyer may speak directly to the other lawyer's client unless the client and the lawyer give their permission, which rarely happens. But *you* can speak directly with the person on the other side. Presumably though, you've already done this without success, which is why there's a lawsuit.

If you really want to settle before the court date, your best chance is to bring in an independent renegotiator—one who isn't a lawyer—to represent you *at any time* during the litigation process. (Most lawyers will advise against this.) The renegotiator can call the other side directly and try to create a settlement out of court.

(This may drive your lawyer crazy, but it's much less hassle, and cheaper than court costs and a lawsuit.)

You can do this whether you're the one who brought the lawsuit, or you're the one being sued. The outcome of any lawsuit is never a given: you may think you have the best case in the world and still lose big. It's always better to settle, even if you receive less than you think you deserve. We all have better things to do in life than to be involved in a lawsuit.

> *Remember that moving on is paramount.*
> *You must believe this for yourself*
> *and sell it to the other party.*

Wherever you find a third party to represent you—whether within your company or an independent contractor—choose wisely. Make sure this person is not attached to particular issues or details of the situation, and will know how to listen to both sides.

Also, make sure the person you choose will speak openly and honestly with you. Don't get a "Yes Person," who will only tell you what you want to hear. A good renegotiator will create an approach that sets the proper tone from the beginning. He or she will understand the secret of the Orange Ball, show respect to all parties, and ensure that your reputation is kept intact. A good renegotiator knows that *it's not just business, it's personal.*

CHAPTER SIX

The Seven Fundamentals of Renegotiating

Over the years, I've developed seven fundamentals for successful renegotiating. These fundamentals should help establish the proper steps you'll need to take to get to a Settlement. You can also use them if you ever find yourself stuck and don't know how to get the renegotiation to move forward. The fundamentals do not follow any particular sequence because their degree of importance varies depending on the nature of the situation.

The Seven Fundamentals are presented on the next page.

The Seven Fundamentals

1. Understand the issues
2. Look for and create opportunities
3. Find a reason
4. Stay honest
5. Find an approach and apply it
6. Recognize attachments
7. Set the right goals

Whether or not things are going smoothly, you can constantly refer back to these to ensure that you stay on track. Whenever you're stuck, come back to a fundamental, see where you are, and decide what you need to do to get to the next step. For example, you may have to adjust your approach (#5) in order to open up or continue the conversation in a productive direction. Or you may need to understand more precisely what the attachments are on both sides (#6), so you can go ahead and remove a particular attachment without a concession on your part.

There are many questions you'll have to ask yourself to clearly determine where you are in the renegotiation process, and what your (or the other party's) position is at any given time. You might be at a point where both sides have agreed they want to find a Solution, but you're still not sure what the other party wants in order to settle.

In the coming pages, I'll also use these fundamentals to help illustrate key differences between negotiating and *re*-negotiating.

I know that I'm repeating myself, but *what matters here is that you identify which fundamentals you must use at any time during the renegotiating process.*

1. Understand the Issues

I chose *Understand the Issues* as the first fundamental because the issues are what distinguish negotiating from *re*-negotiating. Renegotiating, by its very nature, tells you that there is a history between the two parties. And this history automatically reflects a set of issues (for both parties) that existed in the original negotiation, relationship, or agreement.

Several years ago I had an experience that goes to the very heart of understanding the issues. In addition to my renegotiating business, I owned a small call center. We partnered with a company in Long Island that operated call center "seats" in India.

I brought a deal to Steve, the CEO of our Long Island partner company, to sell long-distance phone services to the Indian community in the United States. The only way it made financial sense was to make the sales calls from India. I had a close relationship with the company providing the long distance service (we'll call them Switchtel), and was able to secure a contract in which they provided us with more than 300,000 customer leads in the U.S.

Time passed, and we began to run out of these leads. Switchtel, hoping to provide continued services with another such project, was anxious for us to find a center that could call the Chinese community in the U.S. Soon after, Steve and I found a center in the Philippines that was willing to work with us on the calls to China.

During the four months of the India campaign, we had worked with three different marketing managers at Switchtel. The current marketing manager (MM) had been at her job for only three weeks when we began planning the Chinese call center in the Philippines. She immediately sent me an e-mail requesting that we stop the campaign in India at the end of February.

I didn't understand her reasoning: We were still creating a thousand new customers each month. Although we only had another two weeks' worth of remaining leads, we could still create another 500 or so new customers. The company had been very pleased with our success rate. We'd provided them with over 6,000 new customers in a relatively short period of time.

The following e-mail dialogue shows how a renegotiation can be completely dependent on understanding the issues. The e-mails are between me (Marc) and the marketing manager (MM) on one day at the end of February.

> *Marc:* We're starting the Chinese campaign on March 14th. We're training agents this week and will hire the best. In the meantime we'd like to continue with India. We're still getting 1,000 orders a month. We still have over 50,000 leads and could create another 500 or so new customers. We don't think that's something to throw away.
>
> —
>
> *MM:* Let's get the Chinese program going and worry about the future. I will not consider continuing in India. All calling should stop within three days.
>
> —
>
> *Marc:* We really don't understand why you want to walk away from acquiring these new customers.

Please advise if your director *[I referred to her director by name as I knew her extremely well]* is on the same page. I'd like to speak to her about it. It's also hard to believe you have no more leads, no other call centers calling, and you don't want us to take advantage of every new customer we can bring. I didn't think your company was in the habit of throwing away business.

Please have your director call me. Because you've been copying her on these e-mails, as I have, she should be up to date.

I know I may seem pushy, but when I can't comprehend something and it doesn't make sense to me, I need to pursue it as far as I can. Please forgive me in advance.

—

MM: Marc, I'm completely up-front when it comes to my business relationships. So I'm going to put this out there and chalk it up to developing our relationship.

I am your contact. My director no longer manages your company and I don't need her approval to make business decisions. You need to start developing a relationship with me and leave the past in the past. If I'm going to use you as a call center, I need you to respect my decisions and execute them.

You are *our* vendor, not the other way around. I'm the customer and you don't know what goals and forecasting we've agreed upon internally. Therefore, you're going to have to trust my judgment.

Before I go any further with your company I need to know where you stand. So, I guess I'll put the ball back in your court. If you decide you can respect my business decisions and let me do my job, I look forward to working with you. I'll consider this e-mail a stepping stone in learning how to work with each other. If not, that's fine too.

At this point, Steve called me and said I was going to have to eat humble pie. My reply was "We'll see." It's not that I wanted to be arrogant, or that I was set on being right. I just didn't understand what MM's *issues* were, and she wasn't explaining them. I also didn't think she understood our issues. In a situation like this you can be nice, but still strong. Here's how I responded:

> *Marc:* I understand your position. But remember that I have a long-term relationship with your company. In fact, it was your CEO who recommended that I do business with you.
>
> Even with these relationships, I've never gone behind anyone's back. We've worked with three different Marketing Managers since we began discussions last year regarding the India campaign.
>
> Your Vice President put us in touch with your Director and asked that we work with her. We've always maintained a good relationship with your Director and she's never told us not to contact her if we had any issues, no matter who the Marketing Manager was.
>
> But our history with your company isn't the issue. Our goal was to provide you as many customers as possible from the leads you gave us. As your vendor, one of our jobs is to make you aware when you're leaving profits on the table.
>
> We both need to have patience and learn to work together. The bottom line is that we're all trying to do as much profitable business as possible. We've worked hard for your company on this campaign, and by all accounts we've done a fantastic job. If I didn't honestly know that, this would be a different conversation.
>
> We look forward to fulfilling many more campaigns for your company and Steve and I look forward to working with you.

Steve thought I'd been too strong and had blown the relationship. I didn't think so.

MM never responded by e-mail. The next day she called me to go over some numbers I'd previously requested. She was nice and not at all standoffish. At the end of the conversation, I asked her if we were OK, now that we had had our little tussle. (Remember, I still hadn't received an answer as to why she wanted us to stop the campaign in India. My goal was to be able to continue to get those last 500 orders.) She said she wasn't entirely happy with me.

I told her I'd been married for close to 29 years, and my wife was not completely happy with me either. She laughed and said she could see why.

I told her I wasn't questioning her authority, only her decision. I could not understand why she didn't want us to continue to get another 500 orders. She said she wanted us to start on the Chinese campaign and thought we would lose focus by continuing the campaign in India.

I explained to her that one had nothing to do with the other. The two campaigns were each managed by different people in our organization, one in India and one in the Philippines.

When she understood this she relented. "OK," she said, "Continue in India until you're finished." I said fine, and we moved on. She wanted a completion date and I gave her one. In this the way, we got her another 750 more good customers and she was quite pleased.

This solution did not lie in the details. Actually, the details were confusing the matter.

Details and Issues

Let me clarify the difference between a detail and an issue. In the above story, it may seem that the marketing manager relented once she understood the following detail: that we didn't have the same people handling both call centers. However, I believe the Solution was found when I conveyed to her that I understood her *issue*: to not let the *India* project be disturbed or delayed by the *Chinese* project.

The details only confused the matter until I could clarify the real issue—that there would be no conflict between continuing with the India project and beginning the Chinese project. I also had to get her to understand my issue: there was business being lost if we stopped the India project at that particular time. Once we fleshed out both of our issues, a Solution was found instantly.

> *What is an issue for one party*
> *is not necessarily an issue for the other.*
> *This also holds true for the details.*

Let's simplify the point of understanding the issues. It's crucial for people to clearly identify their real issues: Being right? Winning and getting the better of the other side? Getting the most money?

Whenever I represent someone, the first two questions I try to answer are: What are my client's issues? What are the issues of the other party? Once I know these issues, I can help my client set realistic goals. Take note, however, that no matter what the initial issues are, *you have to allow for the issues to change during the renegotiation process.*

Sometimes I have to change my client's issues so that I can find a Solution to get to a Settlement. For example, if my client tells me, "My biggest issue is to let this company know that we acted correctly, and therefore we will not pay what they think we owe them." This is an issue that won't work.

Instead, I might offer an alternative main issue: "Our relationship has not worked, so let's part ways and move on." My client feels the company did not perform, and as a result, does not want to work with them anymore. The most important thing for my client is to get out of the relationship, and that's it. The money is secondary.

When you get caught up in the money, then the money becomes the issue. Money is always the most difficult issue to resolve. When you make money into the *main* issue and try to resolve that, it hinders the entire renegotiating process. On the other hand, in this example, once you resolve the relationship issue, money issues become relatively simple to resolve.

The other company's representatives, of course, have their own issues. They may feel that they did perform and they just want to get paid. This is fine, but focusing on this isn't going to help them get any more money or settle the relationship.

No one ever wants to be wrong—ever. It's one of the least pleasant situations to be in or to admit to. Being wrong brings up an enormous amount of emotion. This is why finger-pointing (which can be fine in the venting stage) never helps either party to move towards a Solution.

How, then, do you renegotiate with a company that actually did not perform and who really is in the wrong?

Gently! People and companies know when they're wrong and haven't performed, but they don't like to admit it. They prefer to spin the situation to their benefit. Don't make them admit that they're wrong if it doesn't benefit you or lead you to a Solution. They'll appreciate it.

Here is where you can say that some companies just aren't meant to work together. You can make this situation an isolated issue for the company by saying, "I'm sure you have many happy and satisfied customers who believe in your company and appreciate your services. It's time to focus on those customers and build that customer base."

This approach will help them understand that you don't think poorly of them as people or as a company. As a result, they'll be more open to discussing the issues and finding an acceptable way to get out of the relationship.

You've helped them change their issues. It's no longer important for them to prove they're a good company or that they're in the right. When it comes to discussing how much money they deserve, it will be a back and forth discussion until you come to a number that each party is willing to accept. You may have to constantly go back and remind each side what their new issues are, but in my experience you can always find a dollar number that both can live with.

It's important to note here that I did not say "a dollar number that both can be *happy* with." Everyone feels either that they didn't receive enough money or that they paid too much. But that's not the issue.

2. Look for and Create Opportunities

The opportunities for creating a Settlement may not always be obvious at the start of a renegotiation. This is because the opportunities are drawn directly from the issues of each party. Once you identify the issues clearly you'll begin to see exactly what and where the opportunities are.

It may take a little time and patience to flesh out these opportunities. I've talked a lot about the value of listening—opportunities are one of the things you're listening for. And you want to listen carefully because your opportunities will sometimes come in code.

The parties in every renegotiation already have a relationship of some kind—a history. So for a variety of reasons, neither party may be willing to state the obvious. This can make opportunities less apparent. However, it may not always be necessary to explicitly ask people to clarify what they're saying: just make the assumption that you *are* hearing an opportunity. Trust your intuition; it's a powerful tool.

Be creative. Sometimes you can create an opportunity out of nothing, which is fine. You could also be wrong and "create" an opportunity when there isn't one. That's all right as well. Don't worry about it; always try to move forward.

> *Taking what you thought you heard*
> *and using it to create a solution*
> *is what looking for opportunities*
> *is all about.*

Both sides must be willing to listen to you or to each other, if they are dealing directly. This is why setting a positive tone is a key part of creating any opportunity. If you're acting as the renegotiator for someone else, you'll often have to "massage" *both* parties in order to bring them to their respective Comfort Zones.

Sometimes it's good to lay out the opportunities so that each party can recognize all of them, but when you're renegotiating on your own behalf, be cautious when presenting opportunities unless you're offering an unbelievable deal. Remember, your unbelievable deal may not be recognized as being all that unbelievable. This is why it's so important to set the stage prior to discussing the opportunities available for each party. Through continuous conversation opportunities usually become obvious anyway.

For example, what are the opportunities when you're renegotiating a lease?

One option is for the tenant to stop paying and try to force the landlord to make concessions. But then the landlord can just sue and kick out the tenant. But be forewarned: I don't recommend this approach unless you do it *very* carefully. A suit can last three to four months, and is expensive and messy for both sides. There *have* been times when I've threatened this option, however. Initially it angers the landlord, but it also tends to wake him up, hopefully forcing him to expand discussions with me.

Another option is to have the tenant partially pay until the landlord commits to renegotiating or, better yet, until a Solution is found. This is also risky, but it can work if the landlord is unwilling to discuss things with you. Many times, *the opportunities are simply the solutions that have not yet been refined.*

Above all, start with a good attitude. Most people will be open to any opportunity, as wild or crazy as it may sound, if your attitude is good. Approach renegotiations without any feeling of entitlement. If you come to the table feeling you're entitled to something, you'll be talking to a closed ear.

I always tell people they're only entitled to what has been put down in writing in a contract. Tenants often feel they're entitled to a discount, or a change in their lease, simply because the landlord is "making too much money off them." This is ludicrous. If you bring your ego into the equation, no one will want to listen to you. I tell everyone to leave their egos at the door; otherwise, there's nowhere to move.

When you're renegotiating a contract or a relationship, the opportunities are always varied. Let me tell you about a situation that didn't work out too well for me.

Ego, Ego, and More Ego

After years of working for myself, and then several more with a partner, I decided to make a change. I sold my company to my partner and went to work for a larger company, with 200 employees, that did business in nearly every country. I started out as VP of Sales. Instead of being in charge of everything, now I had to answer to superiors. Even though the Chairman was a personal friend, I reported to the CEO and the President.

The company wanted to grow through venture funding and soon hired a new person from the industry to be both CEO and President. After almost a year, the new CEO and his group failed to produce any funding and they were all fired.

I happened to be in Europe with the Chairman at the time. We discussed who should be the next President and COO. The Chairman was set on giving both positions to the VP of Business Development, a very bright guy. But I felt that a single person in the company couldn't and shouldn't do both jobs. I suggested that it would be better if the two responsibilities were split—as is commonly done—between the VP and myself, with both of us reporting to the Chairman.

I got nowhere trying to renegotiate this decision with the Chairman. He told me that the other VP would quit if I were placed in a position over him as COO. I argued that President and COO are at equal levels. The Chairman disagreed, and since he could not afford to lose the other VP, he would not make me the COO. I said that was ridiculous, and threatened to quit if the other VP became President and I didn't become COO.

My approach had two problems: first, the Chairman knew me very well and he knew that I would never leave him when he clearly needed me. Second, I was letting my ego do the arguing. Because I was renegotiating with my ego I couldn't find any opportunities to argue on my behalf in order to achieve my goals. Even though to this day I feel that I was right, I acknowledge that I was arguing with my ego.

The Chairman decided to give me the title of President of Special Operations, reporting directly to him. As it turned out, I actually ended up overseeing virtually all of the operations of the company. This was fine, but everyone knew that I'd been made President of Special Operations only to appease my ego. I learned a valuable lesson.

Though I felt the Chairman was wrong (we argue about it to this day), he made his decision based on his assessment of what was needed for the company. In fact, from a corporate perspective, the Chairman was not wrong. His motives were pure. His goal was to do what was best for the organization. I could not move him in my direction because of my ego. I had the following options: I could either quit, or belly-ache some more (which I did), or just suck it up and move on, which is what I eventually ended up doing.

> *Until you have a settlement,*
> *always keep your eyes open*
> *for more opportunities.*

You don't want to find yourself pinned into a corner before a Settlement has been reached, or at least before a Comfort Zone has been found. Sometimes it's appropriate to follow an opportunity through to its conclusion even though you know it won't work. This gives all parties time to work through their issues and find alternate opportunities. I've seen a lot of people, including me, try to push too quickly for a Solution because they think they know that the final Settlement agreement will end up there anyway.

Both parties need to take their own time to evaluate all their opportunities. Reviewing all of the possible (and even impossible) opportunities will help each party move towards its Comfort Zone.

3. Find a Reason

Among the various opportunities for a Settlement, there is always an underlying reason or rationale—the key ingredient that will help you create a Solution. You must find such a rationale for both sides to deal with each other. To find the reason, you must be quick on your feet and creative in your thinking. What if you encounter someone who is angry and doesn't want to deal? What if everything you say only continues to inflame them? Now you're on the defensive. The reason you're looking for is *that piece of information which allows you to move the renegotiation forward.*

In these situations, I first acknowledge the other party's position, and only then do I begin asking questions. I may say, "I can see that you're very upset and angry, and I understand what you're saying, but if we're going to proceed, I'll need your help."

Then I ask, "If you were I, how would you deal with this situation? What would you like me to say to you, that could improve things?"

Once they begin to answer these questions—no matter what their response is—you've engaged them in a dialogue. And once you've engaged them, you can ask more questions. In their answers lie the opportunities, and in the opportunities lie the reasons—yes, reasons, often many reasons. As a matter of fact, one reason will create another opportunity, which in turn will create another reason. This process will continue, bringing you closer and closer to a final Solution and Settlement.

People tend to vent in hyperbole, making wild statements about what they will or won't do. It's important not to respond, either verbally or emotionally, to such statements. After they've finished, you can simply acknowledge their feelings, but, again, I've found that silence is even better. Listen carefully to what they're saying, because their venting will unintentionally provide you with opportunities and reasons.

---

*Opportunities come when others open up
to you, if you know how to listen.*

When the other side begins to vent or discuss their issues, you've found an opportunity. When they state or intimate that they feel insulted by your client, you've found a reason. Now you know, for example, that they feel they've been mistreated and really want an apology of some kind.

A few years ago I took my two daughters to dinner at Tru, a five-star restaurant in Chicago, to celebrate one daughter's return from France. The meal was one of the best I've ever eaten, and when I got home I recommended Tru to some friends who often visit Chicago and love great restaurants. They came back raving about their meal. My friend's wife even called Tru's management and asked if they would give her a private cooking lesson.

Unfortunately, their response was no, absolutely not. She called and told me what they said. I thought cooking lessons were a great idea and I told her I'd call the restaurant. She said not to bother; they were adamant about not doing it.

I knew that I had to come up with a different way of communicating to Tru's management in order to get a different response. I asked my friend to tell me everything she'd said to them, and what their excuses had been for not agreeing.

In their response to her I discovered how to approach them. The manager's comments had been: "We just don't do this kind of thing." He also said that he hadn't even asked the Chef about the request. This was it. This was the key I could use, first to convince the manager to ask the Chef, and second, to ask the Chef in a manner that would elicit a positive response.

When I called the manager to discuss the idea, he again refused. They just weren't interested. I asked him for his reasons why they didn't want to do it. He gave me a long list, including the fact that they'd never done anything like this before for non-professionals. I wrote the list down as he was speaking, and when he was done I said, "If it were possible for me to satisfy you on each point you just made, would you then consider arranging for a lesson?" He said he'd be interested in hearing my rebuttal.

Now he was having a bit of fun with me and we had an exchange going on. But he had also opened the door for me to repudiate all of his reasons for saying no. I proceeded to give him an alternative to each point, except for one, which I couldn't figure out. "This reason is too difficult for me," I said. "Do you have any suggestions?"

Without pausing, he immediately came up with an answer to his own argument that I never would have thought of. Here was the angle: getting him to help me refute his own argument. He laughed, "Wait a minute, I'm not supposed to be arguing your side!"

I told him that this proved to me that he really wanted to offer the cooking lessons. He just had to have good reasons for it.

In the end we made a deal. Seven of us, including one of my daughters and another friend's son, went there for a two-day course and an amazing meal. We had lots of fun and learned a great deal. I can tell you that Tru's staff works really hard and has a grand passion for what they do. I highly recommend Tru if you're ever in Chicago. I've been back twice by myself to get instructions on specific dishes I wanted to learn, and they've been very accommodating.

My friend's son was so inspired by the lessons at Tru that he decided to enroll in cooking school.

When renegotiating anything, be persistent. Remember what Churchill said: "Never give up. Never give up. Never give up. Never, never, never give up!"

Looking for the right reason is critical, but you may need to use more than one reason to get to a Solution. Remember, *all roads lead to Rome*. There are many roads that can lead you to a Solution and on to a Settlement. Don't be attached to any one path or any one reason. Your success may depend on your flexibility and creativity.

If you get stuck at some point during a renegotiation, it's OK to say, "I'd like to think about everything you've said today, and I'll come back to you in few days with a response. I respect the points you've brought up, and I want to do justice to them by spending some time thinking about them. I'll call you back in the next day or two. Thank you very much for your time and candor. It's been quite helpful."

Then do it. Take some time to think. Discuss the points with your colleagues, or if you're not representing yourself, with your client. Write down alternative ways to respond. Look for opportunities in whatever was said to you. Find a reason to move the conversation or deal forward. There are no fixed rules here. You don't have to solve the issues all in one conversation; don't even try. Just make sure you're always moving forward. Sometimes you may have to take a few steps backward to eventually move forward.

4. Stay Honest

Staying honest is about the manner in which you present your or your client's situation and the need to renegotiate. It's imperative that you stay honest throughout the renegotiation process. Of course, being honest is vital to any relationship—honesty conveys respect, and when we give respect, we get respect.

I've represented several clients who didn't have an honest complaint, but they did have real issues from their side. They had no problem with the entity with whom they had the contract or relationship, but the time had come to make changes to the contract, or simply to alter the relationship in some way.

These sorts of scenarios don't mean that you cannot, or should not, renegotiate the deal—only that you must be very careful. My suggestion is to be very open and honest when presenting your or your client's reasoning. If you aren't, the other party will see through you no matter what you do, so you might as well be up-front from the beginning. Being honest is about being forthright and direct, and not trying to spin something that isn't true.

Real estate contracts are particularly good examples of the need for an honest approach. The first thing you should know is that real estate contracts are almost always well-written. Most individuals or companies who enter into these contracts make sure that all of their bases are covered before they sign. As I've mentioned before, unless a landlord violated the terms of the lease, there's rarely a legal reason to get him to renegotiate. If you try to lie about or spin your situation, the landlord will find out and then not want to help you. It's much better just to be honest when approaching landlords, because they'll be that much more receptive to your situation.

In other types of contract renegotiations you have to find honest reasons not only to get someone to speak with you, but also to engage you in conversation that will move towards a Solution, and ultimately, a Settlement. Let's say that for one reason or another, your client can't seem to get its relationship with another company to work. When you first approach the other company, you must discover what the experience has been like for them. If the experience is bad for one party, it's usually not so good for the other one.

After you listen, you can tell them that your client's experience has not been a good one. Tell them your client feels he or she has made every effort to make the relationship work, but has not succeeded. Your personal integrity is at stake here, so it's critically important to develop a perspective that sheds an honest light on your position. At this point you've been honest and open with the other side, and now they must decide how to respond.

Just Ask

A store-owner friend of mine once over-bought from two of her vendors. As a result, she wanted the vendors to help her on the next orders by agreeing either to accept a late payment or to reduce the order.

She considered herself one of their best customers and had never before asked for special treatment. But the vendor companies wouldn't agree. They refused to cancel her order, and they wouldn't allow her to pay late. Frustrated, my friend asked me to call the vendors and speak to them on her behalf.

When I called each company I asked them to explain their position. They both explained that they were small companies and couldn't afford cancellations or late payments. I was completely honest and told them that my friend had seriously over-bought for the spring season, and now needed help for the fall season. They both told me that my friend needed to order more conservatively and shouldn't expect them to help if she over-bought.

My friend and I agreed with their analysis, but she still needed their help. I assured the companies that this would never happen again, and asked if they could help her out in some way. I was completely forthright, and that allowed us to quickly get to the real issues. In the end, they accepted the situation because my friend wasn't necessarily the only one at fault: they may have oversold her.

Equally important, I wasn't trying to blame them for any of my friend's problems. I just pointed out that they had a good customer who needed their help. They both agreed to help her out, and all parties were happy in the end. The companies also felt they'd done the right thing by aiding a loyal customer.

Always maintain high ethical standards regardless of the actions of those around you.

The Art Collector

A couple of years ago, I had a client who is an art dealer (call him Rob). He had an opportunity to represent and advise a businessman (Doug) on specific pieces of art from a collection in Europe. Rob and Doug signed an agreement in which Rob would introduce Doug to a famous collector in Germany. The deal stated that Rob would receive 10% of the purchase price of anything Doug bought from the German art collector.

My client Rob accompanied Doug and Doug's associate to Germany to introduce the collector and give advice on which pieces Doug should buy and at what price. Doug purchased two pieces of art on the spot.

He then decided to renegotiate his deal with Rob and pay him only 5% instead of 10%, even though a 10% commission is standard in the industry. Rob accepted this new proposal for two reasons. He thought $80,000 (the total of a 5% commission on the two current purchases) was a decent amount of money based on his efforts, and he felt certain he would earn other commissions on Doug's future purchases.

Doug returned to the U.S. and, through his own associate, proceeded to purchase another $3.5 million in artwork from the same German collector. When Rob learned of these purchases he contacted Doug to receive his commission. Doug refused to pay. When Rob asked why, he replied, "Because I don't want to."

A year went by. Rob found me through a mutual friend, and asked if I would represent him and collect the money. I told him that I wasn't a bill collector, but that I would speak to Doug and try to renegotiate the contract so we could find a Solution and a Settlement.

Rob had very little documentation to support his position. I asked him to send me a copy of his contract. It turned out to be a handwritten agreement that really didn't say anything except that Rob would introduce Doug to the art collector in Germany and mentioned that the "Art Dealer" was entitled to a 10% commission. The agreement did not discuss the details of what constituted a purchase, or any criteria for the quality or value of the painting purchased. It was a weak contract for both parties.

When I checked up on Doug, I was told that he was very wealthy and very tough to deal with. This did not deter me. I called and told him, "I represent Rob; however I'm not a lawyer or a bill collector. I understand there's an issue about the commission." Doug's response was that he hadn't bought any additional paintings since his original purchase through Rob, and he didn't owe Rob a nickel. (He had paid Rob his commission for the original purchase.) He said that Rob had given him very bad advice, and as a result, he'd lost money on what he did buy.

I learned from Rob that Doug's associate had purchased a piece of artwork for him for $2 million, and later Doug lost $400,000 when it was sold at Christies. I now knew that Doug had lied to me when he said that he hadn't bought anything else. Doug's position was that he didn't owe Rob anything because the artwork in question had been bought through an associate, and not by Doug himself. At the same time, Doug wouldn't admit having bought anything else. He was quite clearly contradicting himself.

I asked Rob if he had given poor advice, and he didn't have a good answer. He admitted that Doug may have paid a little too much, but he thought that had nothing to do with his outstanding commission. The contract made no mention of payments being based on good or bad advice. The contract did state the commission was owed regardless of who bought the artwork—friend, relative, or associate.

Here's the text of their inadequate contract:

> Doug or X, hereby agrees to pay Rob or Y an introduction commission of 10% of the purchase price of any and all paintings purchased by X or his partner and/or agents as a result of his introduction by Y to numerous paintings of artist's name or Z and other important 16th and 17th century paintings in a

private collection in Germany. Information on this collection has been communicated to X by Y and photographs have been FedEx'ed to X by Y.

Rob and Doug signed, and it was done. Lawyers may be difficult to deal with, and may not be good negotiators or renegotiators, but they can write good contracts that protect both parties. I told Doug he should have known better than to enter into this contract. He should have used his in-house counsel. I told both parties that this was the dumbest contract I'd ever seen, for both sides.

I had to find the answers to the following questions: Does Rob have an honest complaint? Is he entitled to his commission? If Doug did get bad advice and if in fact he did lose a large sum of money, should he have to pay the commission?

A good contract is essential. This contract only stated that Doug has to pay the commission if the artwork is purchased. Rob is setting himself up as an expert and advising Doug on what price he should pay. Does this make Rob responsible for Doug's losses? Unless Rob had lied about the value and inflated the price so he could get a higher commission, I didn't see why Rob would be liable for Doug's loss. Nor could it be proved that Rob knew the paintings were overpriced.

To get paid, Rob first needed to verify the purchases. In my investigation, I received very good verbal proof from an art dealer in London that Doug, through an associate, had indeed purchased the painting for $2 million, in addition to another painting for $350,000. Rob, who was on his way to Europe, told me that he would go to Germany and obtain written confirmation of the purchases from the collector.

I developed a very good relationship with Doug. He was easy to work with. He never avoided my calls and our conversations were always cordial. Even when we disagreed, he was pleasant. He knew that I was being honest with him, but he was going to make me work for any money I was going to get out of him. He had done some checking on me and learned I was tough but fair, and once I started a project I wouldn't let go until I had a Settlement.

Doug could also be difficult, however. He wouldn't admit to buying any artwork, and continued to say that he wasn't responsible for someone else's purchase. He knew very well that I wasn't going away, but he wasn't afraid of being sued.

He asked for a copy of the contract. I faxed it to him and he showed it to his own in-house lawyer. He offered us $5,000 over the phone, to go away. I laughed and told him it was an insult. Take it, he said, or sue me. I said OK, we'll speak later. Doug understood very well that he might owe us more, but he just didn't feel we had a legitimate claim. He was also very angry with Rob for giving him bad advice. I needed more proof.

After months of waiting, we still hadn't received written documentation from the German art collector, though he had said he would provide it. At this point I was so disappointed with Rob and how he handled the situation that I was becoming fed up. He hadn't been very clear or honest with me. Even though Doug had actually lied to me, I liked him better than Rob. The details didn't matter to Doug. He felt the deal had cost him and he didn't want to pay any more unless he was forced to. We would have had a Solution if Doug knew that we had real proof that he had bought the additional artwork.

I'm sorry to say that this was never settled. It is an example of an unsuccessful renegotiation, but it's also a great example of how to get cooperation from someone who doesn't want to cooperate, simply by using honesty as the basis of renegotiating. That Doug got away without paying any commission is not the point. Because I presented Rob's position in an honest way, I developed a rapport with Doug, and he told me what I had to do if I expected to get money out of him.

Staying honest is essential whenever your integrity and reputation are at stake: in other words, in any renegotiation. People on both sides almost always know when you're lying or spinning a story to suit your position. The problem with lying or spinning the truth is you never know when you're going to get caught. But it will catch up with you. If your clients ever ask you to lie on their behalf, don't do it; it's not worth it. The truth creates a better story anyway, and gives you an angle to get to a Solution.

If you find out that your client has lied to you—it happens—you'll have to figure out how to tell the other party in a way that doesn't shut down the renegotiations. The other side will probably become angry, but they'll appreciate your honesty and may well continue to work with you to reach a Settlement. In the end, however, it will most likely cost your client something.

One more point: you may not have to inform the other party about your client's dishonesty if it's not pertinent to the renegotiating. This will be your judgment call.

Being honest and up-front gives you great credibility. When you renegotiate a contract that clearly states the positions of both parties, you're not implying wrongdoing by either party. You, your company, or your client may still need relief from a contract *even though you don't have a claim.* In the end, you can still renegotiate the contract; it may just cost you more. Remember, money is not always the issue.

5. Find an Approach and Apply It

Your approach starts from the moment you begin a conversation. It begins with the tone and content of the first words that come out of your mouth. If you start negatively, you'll get a negative response. If you start positively, you can get a neutral or positive response. I say "can," because there are times when you'll get a negative response no matter what you say. But if so, *your response* to this negativity will set the tone of the renegotiation.

Be careful here. Listen to the details, but respond positively no matter what's being said. The tone and the details you're listening to are not to be taken personally. Again, behave as if it's personal, but *react* as if it's business.

> *Your approach will dictate*
> *the prevailing mood*
> *of the entire renegotiating process.*

This is why your approach must provide each party with an opportunity to open up to you so they can honestly discuss the issues. The success of your approach has everything to do with your ability to communicate.

Those you speak with must understand that your intention in the first conversation is only to listen. Your goal is to perceive the mood and the issues of the relationship. Your approach sets this in motion. A successful approach will get all parties on the same page, allowing you to focus on the issues that are important for creating a Solution, hence, transcending those details that will only bog you down.

The following is an approach I often use. It allows people to quickly open up to me.

"Hello, I'm Marc Freeman, and I represent XYZ Company. I'd like to start out by saying that I'm not a lawyer. I'm just someone who helps companies renegotiate contracts. I understand that you have a contract with XYZ Company, and they've asked me to call you to discuss this contract. I want you to know that I've asked XYZ not to tell me all the details of the agreement they want to renegotiate with you. In this way I can hear from you—without any preconceived judgments on my part—what's happened so far. I'd love to hear your assessment of the relationship, and why you think XYZ would want to renegotiate."

This approach immediately tells the other party two things: 1) I'm someone who will listen to them; and 2) I won't automatically take the side of my client. This is critical. After all, my client could be in the wrong. My client could have behaved unfairly, or not lived up to his or her side of the commitment. This approach is also a good way to establish the facts without beating around the bush or starting with an argument.

Never try to *settle* the issue with your approach. Your approach should simply open up the conversation, so that you can begin the renegotiation on a positive note. "A positive note" means willingness on the part of the other party to discuss the issues with you.

Every time you begin a new conversation, you have another opportunity to create an approach. You may decide to keep the same approach, or you may want to change it based on the last conversation. *Never begin a conversation by being belligerent or angry, making accusations, or acting "entitled." Always ease into the conversation, being open and nice.*

> To be a good communicator
> you must be a good listener.

Before you get off the phone, be sure the person on the other end understands what you've just said. You may even have to ask them to repeat your points back to you. And don't be embarrassed to repeat what you just said in order to clarify yourself. Successful communication has a great deal to do with your intentions, your tone of voice, and the approach you use.

Sometimes I use humor in my approach just to put everyone at ease. It's critical, though, that any humorous comment you make is actually funny. Otherwise, there could be a big "thud" on the other end of the phone. Worse, if the other person doesn't think you're funny, it could even work against you.

Later in this chapter you will see that I once opened a conversation with the owner of a company that was suing us, by saying, "You must be extremely angry with us." I said this with a little chuckle and sarcasm in my voice. I knew he was quite angry with us. This got him off guard. He didn't expect it, but was happy to have the opportunity to speak openly and honestly with someone who would listen to him.

Who is at fault if your approach conveys something other than what you intend? Probably you are. You have to be clear enough so your listeners understand what you're saying, as you intended to say it. Being clear is critical.

Every year after the President gives his State of the Union Address, all the political pundits gather around and discuss what they think he said and meant. Every year there are as many opinions of what he said, and meant to say, as there are pundits; maybe more. I always laugh when the press says the President and Congress don't agree. I adore my children and they love me, yet our family often doesn't agree. Why is it such a surprise that a large group of powerful and influential people, each with his or her own agenda, do not agree with one another?

Poorly Made Gift Sets

One factory in China we worked with, prior to opening our own factory, printed our stationery pieces—envelopes, note cards, and writing paper—and assembled our stationery baskets. The baskets themselves, along with pens and other items that went into them, were shipped in from other factories for assembly. At one point, we sub-contracted this factory to assemble a different product—our bath gift baskets. According to our agreement, the factory was to ship both types of assembled baskets within a specific time frame.

During a routine inspection, we discovered that both the assembled bath and stationary baskets were of poor quality, and the factory would not be able to meet the shipping deadline. The lack of quality was in the assembly itself—the baskets just weren't put together very well. It was also clear that the factory wasn't producing baskets fast enough to ship on time.

We talked with the factory owners and they said they'd gotten behind, but would catch up and be more careful with the quality. But they ended up shipping the first half of the order late, and the quality really didn't improve. The second half of the order was late as well.

As a result, our customer had to mark down the retail price, and asked us to pay for the mark-down. We had no choice, and lost our profit and more. The factory, of course, wanted to be paid in full, while we wanted a discount for all the problems we felt they had created.

My partner and I set up a meeting to discuss the situation with the three brothers who owned the factory. We'd been to many meetings like this and had already decided not to use this factory in the future, so we were in a better position for renegotiation. It was important, however, that we create a situation that would not leave any issues remaining after the settlement.

Our reputation was important to us. We didn't want the factory owners saying negative things about us to other factories. Also, we had a close personal history with the owners: we had socialized with them and their families on several occasions.

On the way to the meeting my partner and I decided on what we thought was a fair discount given the circumstances, and what approach we would take. We decided to keep it simple—just explain the facts. Since we'd been quite close to the three owners, we knew they could push our buttons. My partner asked me not to lose my temper. I agreed to control myself if my partner could agree to control himself. He then bet me $20 I'd lose my temper before he did. I took the bet.

I began the meeting with the owners by explaining our situation, emphasizing that we wanted to be honest and up-front. I talked about the commitments they'd made and didn't keep, and all of the money we'd invested and lost. About an hour and a half into the meeting, the brothers were still saying they expected us to pay in full, and were asking when they could expect our payment!

We were shocked that they would not take any financial responsibility. Again we calmly tried to communicate our position, but the results were no different. After a while my partner became frustrated. He stood up, handed me a $20 bill, and began to scream at the brothers. I didn't blame him, but for some reason I was able to hang on a bit longer. Eventually my partner calmed down and we decided to take a break.

During the break my partner and I discussed what we were doing wrong, and why the brothers weren't getting it. We realized that we had done all the talking and hadn't listened to them at all. Our approach was miscalculated: a good approach must take into account the listening portion of the discussion after you've made your initial presentation. We should have asked them to explain their side first.

We decided to go back in and just listen. First, my partner apologized for his outburst and for not really listening to what they had to say. We asked them to discuss the whole situation from their point of view.

They began by saying they had worked very hard to comply with our need to ship a good quality order on time. However, they felt we'd asked them to do a job that was more than they could handle. They hadn't realized how difficult it would be. But they felt *we* should have known it was beyond their capabilities, and therefore it was primarily our fault. They were very proud of their factory and the quality of their work.

We responded by agreeing that they ran a great factory, which is why we chose to work with them in the first place. We also agreed that the project might have been more difficult than everyone had anticipated.

At this point in the meeting, my partner and I realized the Solution was not in the details, but in the fact that they were extremely proud of their factory. Their main issue was not wanting anyone to think negatively about their factory. If we paid them anything less than the full amount, it would be like admitting their factory wasn't very good. But in spite of this, of course, we still wanted some kind of discount.

We told them we fully understood their position, and they were one hundred percent correct. We also explained that the situation was very difficult for us because we'd lost so much money on this project. We offered the following proposal: if we admitted that it was partially our fault, would they take some responsibility for accepting a project for which they were unprepared? We emphasized that this did not reflect on their factory as a whole, only on their judgment on this particular deal. We said we wanted to remain friends and assured them we would speak highly of them. We also told them if we ever had a project that was a better fit, we would bring it to them and decide together if the project could be profitable for them.

On this basis, we asked the brothers for a discount on the project under discussion. We had found a Solution and could finally get to the Comfort Zone, where we discussed the exact amount of the discount. In the end we didn't get quite as high a discount as we wanted, but it was within five percent, which was a good Comfort Zone for us and acceptable to them.

My partner and I learned a valuable lesson about renegotiating. Going into a situation and presenting your needs and position first often works to your disadvantage; this is not a good approach.

Frequently, we find ourselves saying one thing, thinking another, and intending something completely different. In the renegotiation process you must be clear. Your approach will help you set the stage for that clarity. Don't be surprised if someone doesn't understand what you're saying in the way you intended it. Be patient, and check from time to time to be sure that everyone is on the same page. If not, keep rephrasing what you're saying until you feel satisfied you're being understood.

It's perfectly acceptable to ask questions of the other party so you can be sure you're being clear. It may be that your approach is actually preventing others from understanding you. If this is the case, stop, take a breath, and change your approach. Changing your approach mid-stream in such circumstances is evidence of being flexible and using creative business sense.

6. Recognize Attachments

Getting along with people can be a challenge. This is why creating a relationship with those with whom you are renegotiating has to be carefully developed. You must understand from the outset that you're not going to like everyone you deal with, and vice versa.

Even though you may know the other person and already have a relationship, you still need to be careful not to take anything for granted. You never know how someone might react when you need to break a promise or commitment. Don't make assumptions about how they may or may not act.

This is why your approach is always critical. This is just a fact. The issue is not whether you *like* the individual(s) you're dealing with. If it is, then you'll become an issue yourself, and therefore the wrong person to be doing the renegotiating. You'll defeat your own purpose.

In my call center business I dealt with a client's marketing director, whom I discussed earlier in the section on Fundamental #1 (*Understand the Issues*). I knew she didn't particularly like me because I kept asking her if her boss and boss's boss agreed with her decisions (I had been working with them before I met her). Although I never actually went over her head, this drove her crazy, and I knew it.

She continually made decisions, however, that I believed were arbitrary and not in the best interest of either her company or mine. I just would not accept her word. Whether or not I liked her as a person was immaterial. I didn't have to like her—I needed a working relationship with her so she would continue to use our services. As I told her one day in a rather heated conversation, "We can work together and still not see eye to eye on every issue."

Even though she agreed, it was important for me that she not be so attached to her point of view. I knew she was quite inexperienced; this was in fact her first managerial position. She was attached to being right, and also to being in control whether she was right or wrong. This kind of attachment would make any renegotiation a little sticky.

Make sure those you are dealing with understand that even though you may be attached to your own point of view—*i.e.,* you feel it is a non-negotiable point—you're still willing to listen to other perspectives. Ideally, however, the other party shouldn't see you as being attached to *any* particular point of view.

Don't tip your hand by giving up too much information. Don't get ahead of yourself. For example, if someone you're renegotiating with says that all you want is a discount on what your client owes, you can reply, "This is what they *want*, but first you and I need to discuss whether or not they actually deserve a discount, right?"

In this way you've prepared the ground, and you can begin to discuss the issues. You'll learn from these discussions which points they're attached to. They probably already know you're attached to some kind of discount. That's not important as long as they don't think you're attached to any *specific amount* of discount.

These attachments, both theirs and yours, are critical because they provide the opportunities you need to find a Solution. Remember: *both* parties must go beyond *all of the attachments*—theirs and yours (or your client's)—to create a settlement. Creating a good working relationship will override much of the need for the other party to hold on to small details that can prevent you from finding a Solution.

Whenever I spoke with the marketing director of that telecom company, I tried to end on a warm or lighthearted note. This is an important component of your approach. Never, if it's at all possible, end a phone call or face-to-face conversation when you or the other party is angry. Otherwise, that anger will be carried over into your next conversation or meeting.

Anger is a red flag indicating that someone is too attached to his or her point of view. Being attached to a certain point of view isn't necessarily bad, but if the other side sees your attachment early on in the renegotiations, they'll feel trapped without much room to maneuver, and they'll dig in. Although nobody can help being attached to something now and then, the trick is not to let the other side know how attached you are.

The best renegotiations occur when the other party doesn't imagine you're attached to any particular point of view. This gives you power during the process. You'll be in control of the direction of the renegotiation, and you will have the Orange Ball.

Attachments Lead to Deal-Breakers

I've said that "being attached" occurs when you, or your client, have a particular point which is definitely not negotiable. On rare occasions it may be important as a courtesy to let the other party know this up front. But do so *only* if giving up this information is beneficial to the process. *Get all of the deal breakers—the non-negotiable points—on the table as soon as possible.* I realize this is a big contradiction to what I said in the paragraphs above. But trust me, there are times when it can be quite useful to let those you're renegotiating with know what points are *not* negotiable, right at the beginning of the process.

You have to be the judge of when it's appropriate to express the non-negotiable points and when it's better to keep them quiet. Even though some points may be non-negotiable, never seem adamant about them. You may discover, as the renegotiation proceeds, that you're not as attached to them as you originally thought. Also, the person you're dealing with may find a way around your non-negotiable point that you hadn't thought of. You certainly don't want to hold on to a point just for the sake of it.

I had a client who was adamant about reducing the cost of their lease but didn't want to move from their current space. The client thought the business might grow again and they would need the space. They also felt the prestige of their current space was perfect for their relationships with their clients. They also believed the cost of moving would eat up the savings they'd get from the reduced rent. Accordingly, they told me I could renegotiate anything but they wouldn't move.

When I spoke to the landlord, I said one of the conditions for my client was that they really would prefer to stay in the same space. I didn't mention they were adamant, nor did I suggest it wasn't negotiable. I left it as an open, but desired, condition. I didn't feel my client was in a position to make too many demands—reducing the rent was a big enough demand as it was.

The landlord's representative was a terrific guy. He knew the client didn't want to move, but he came up with a solution that put them into a new space which suited them well and gave them a reduction in rent that more than covered the cost of the move. In the end, both parties were reasonably satisfied.

> *A deal-breaker at the beginning of the renegotiation is not necessarily a deal-breaker at the end.*

Once both parties understand the obstacles, you can work around them more effectively (in this case, negotiators from both sides). Also, what is non-negotiable in the beginning of the discussions may very well become a negotiable point later on, when all the issues and needs have been clearly expressed by all parties.

Not every conversation during a renegotiation will go smoothly or result in agreement. This is normal and OK. It's like making bread. You have to knead the dough, let it sit and rise for a time, and then knead it again before baking it. Points of attachment (like dough) need to be expressed and acknowledged (kneaded) and the process needs time for development. It requires careful attention and patience.

The goal of each conversation should be to establish at least *one point of agreement* between the parties even if it's only that you both agree to think about what was discussed and get back to each other in a couple of days.

Sometimes it's important to allow the other person to have the upper hand for a while. Let them think that you may be willing to accept the points they're attached to. (We talked about this in chapter two, *The Secret of the Orange Ball.*) Also, keep in mind that you don't always have to be serious. Create some lightness. Don't make every conversation life or death, or every point a deal breaker.

Above all, listen. I can't say it enough. The person you're dealing with, creating a relationship with, must trust that you're really listening. And the more upset or angry that person is, the more important it is to listen.

Ask a lot of questions, especially about the points they seem to be most attached to. Be direct. Ask why a particular point is so important to them. You may find valuable opportunities in their answer. Remember how attached that marketing director was for us to finish the phone campaign in India before we started the Chinese campaign? That was because she *did not understand* we were using separate call centers for the two projects and one had nothing to do with the other. Once she understood this, she allowed us to finish the Indian campaign.

Another reason to ask questions is to be sure you completely understand their points. *It may seem like a truism to you (or a revelation), but many people don't say what they really mean.* Only through questioning can you discover what they're actually saying, and what their attachments are.

Their real attachment may have nothing to do with the point they're discussing. Or, this point may not be *their* attachment; it may be their boss's attachment or that of someone else in their organization. In this case the person you're talking to may be able to help you, or even become your ally, as you work through that attachment. Remember the manager of the restaurant, Tru, and how he helped me through one of the attachments? When I had asked him how he would answer a particular objection, he gave me a rather credible answer. Having done so, he then realized he really wasn't that attached to this point after all.

The course of any renegotiation is always changing. Be aware that different points of attachment will crop up during the process. Don't be alarmed if the other party, or your own client, suddenly identifies some new issue they hadn't realized they were attached to. If you're honest and forthright you should be able to work through any point of attachment with anyone at any time.

Listening is your best tool to help you work through all the points of attachment and get the renegotiation on the right track.

7. Set the Right Goals

The goals for both sides can *and will* change throughout the re-negotiation. What's more, goals vary from person to person and company to company. Clarifying the goals only happens after all the issues are understood.

The one unchanging and ultimate goal for any renegotiation should be to "move on." Many times we don't realize the hidden costs in employee hours, money, and psychology to a company that is in a relationship or contract which isn't working. Any dysfunctional re-lationship or contract (even if it isn't a drain on specific resources) is certainly not generating profit or benefit for the company. This is why *moving on* is always the biggest issue and greatest goal.

Goals should be specific to the issues—the more specific the better. Simply asserting that a Solution or Settlement needs to be achieved doesn't constitute a valid goal. Before beginning the renegotiation, you must create realistic goals to give yourself or your client a par-ticular direction. Note, however, that if your initial goals are too specific, you may become too attached to them, and this could pre-vent you from making changes and moving on.

The degree to which you need or want to move on will help you create your goals. *Move on at what cost?* What are you willing to give up to get this problem out of your life? Remember, any two companies who are trying to get out of their relationship with each other will have different goals.

As the renegotiator, one of your tasks is to help your clients clarify their goals. But there have been times when I was able to help the other party do this as well. This is a good thing to do; it will ad-vance your search for both a Common Ground and a Solution. Of course, the best-case scenario is when both sides have similar goals. Initially, I try to convince both sides that their main goal is shared: to move on. Once this is established, it's easier to set other goals and to find a Solution. The more experienced I become, the more I believe in *moving on* as a key goal.

It takes time and patience to achieve goals, and getting there can be a circuitous road. Clarifying the goals on both sides of the renegotiation process can take time. And it is a process.

The renegotiating process will often come to a standstill, and this is a good time for your clients to reevaluate their goals. Ask them, "What do you really want and need from this renegotiation?" If you have already helped your clients establish "moving on" as the ultimate goal, remind them of this. (Be sure to make this point often with the other side as well.) This will create more flexibility for all parties to move away from the issues that they seem most attached to. As long as you're being fair to your side, you should eventually get the other side to bend.

It's like taking a long trip; if you always focus on where you want to end up, you won't be able to enjoy the scenery along the way. That's right, *enjoy*. The process of renegotiating can, and should, be a good experience for both parties. Even if it's difficult, or the parties are angry with one another in the beginning, there will still be opportunities for a good experience. Identifying and understanding all the issues, and then clarifying the goals so that you can create a Solution and a Settlement, will give everyone a great feeling of accomplishment.

As I quoted earlier, "All sales success depends on how many 'no's' you can take." The salesperson who can take the most "no's" is the one who gets the most sales. Successful renegotiating depends on how many times you can hear the other party say, "No, I'm not going to budge from my position."

I respond to that by continually coming back with a new idea for how to resolve the issue. (Persistence. Persistence. Persistence.) Try to introduce different goals, possibly smaller ones.

> *It's good to break large goals into smaller ones to help the parties move on.*

Not Everything Is Possible

There are times, though, when things just don't work out—impossible situations, or impossible people.

I had a client, an older woman, who had been taken advantage of by some real estate developers in Northern California. She had a judgment from the courts for one million dollars, but the developers refused to pay her. Somehow they were able to hide their assets so that, even though she had the law on her side and a judgment against them for a specific sum, her attorneys couldn't get her the money she was owed. She wanted me to attempt to pry some money out of the developers. She had tried and tried. She had hired several different lawyers; I was her last chance.

I called the people who owed her the money and we had a very long, pleasant conversation. They *seemed* nice, but they were unwilling to pay the woman anything. I called them back every week for two months. At the very least, I wanted to make them feel guilty for suckering this elderly woman out of her life savings and leaving her with nothing for her retirement. But they simply did not care.

I finally blew up and told them, "What goes around comes around, and I hope I live long enough to see you get yours!" I was very angry, but what could I do? They were not good people. They were only concerned with their goals, not anyone else's, and this "justified" twisting all their actions to their own benefit. The situation disgusted me. I just had to move on, which I did. But I still feel bad that I couldn't convince these people to do anything. (The only thing I was able to do for her was not to charge for my services.)

In the end, both you and the other party must have clear, fair goals. Eventually, those goals will merge. If not, it will be difficult to find a Solution or create a Settlement. Again, moving on is everyone's reward.

I've often said that during any renegotiation process "there are no mistakes, only wrong turns." In other, words, don't worry about making a mistake as long as you treat people with respect. If you see that you've inadvertently said or done something to offend the person you're dealing with, just apologize and know that you made a wrong turn but you can get back on track. Refer back to these seven fundamentals and they will set you straight again. Remember to keep your intentions pure and you will be all right.

CHAPTER SEVEN

Five Types of Renegotiations

Now that we have a structured view of renegotiating, including the Five Principles, the ten-point Checklist, and the Seven Fundamentals, let's take a closer look at how they apply to specific types of contracts and agreements. Of course, you can apply each principle or fundamental in every renegotiation, but some are more relevant than others in certain types of agreements, contracts, or commitments.

I've broken down all kinds of renegotiation into five basic categories listed on the next page. These should cover ninety-five percent of the situations you might find yourself dealing with.

Five Types of Renegotiations

1. Real estate:
   lease renegotiations and buyouts

2. Contract renegotiations and buyouts

3. Contract collections

4. Restructuring debt:
   accounts payable & accounts receivable

5. Personal contracts

1. Real Estate Lease Renegotiations and Buyouts

Real estate leases are among the most difficult contracts to renegotiate. They're *always* written to benefit the landlord, so unless a landlord is in breach of the lease agreement, all the legal points have been crafted to his or her advantage. This is why renegotiating a real estate lease is rarely, if ever, in the landlord's best interest; a landlord is almost never legally bound to do so.

You must have a significant reason if you want a landlord to even consider a proposal of renegotiation. Furthermore, if your attitude is that the landlord is gouging you and doesn't really deserve to be paid, you're guaranteed to get nowhere. Since you or your client signed the lease, you're obligated to perform in accordance with it.

If you didn't like the terms from the beginning, you shouldn't have signed the lease.

On the other hand, what if your business has recently taken a downturn and you simply don't need as much space? In a situation like that, you must be able to provide accounting documentation to show the landlord that if, for example, you continue at the current rent with the current space, you'll eventually be put out of business. This *is* a compelling reason for a landlord to renegotiate.

What principles and fundamentals are best used in this situation? In every case it will be about gaining control of the Orange Ball. The fifth fundamental—*find an approach and apply it*—is critical here, because your approach will set the tone for controlling the Orange Ball. But the best approach overall is to be straightforward and honest; I've found that nothing else really works.

Having patience is also incredibly important. Don't try to get an answer in the first conversation. Explain to the landlord exactly what you need and why, and then ask your landlord to think about it and arrange another time to meet.

Sometimes your landlord will try to give you an answer right then and there. If you do get a positive response, then that's great. But if your landlord turns you down, ask him or her to think about it for a few days.

Occasionally, a landlord will maintain that there is nothing else to speak about: his decision is final. Here, although you may be upset and angry, you need to push the Refresh Button. Stay nice, and be respectful. Ask the landlord to meet in a few days, because *you* need time to think about this response. And always, thank him or her for considering your situation.

The next time you meet with the landlord you need to remember the fourth fundamental: *stay honest*. Don't come back and change your story, or spin a story to try to get the landlord to budge. Just keep working on the landlord by listening carefully to everything he says and asking a lot of questions.

Informed Compromise

I recently represented a client who was losing money every month. His company needed some relief, but he didn't want to give up his office space, because he knew his company could eventually grow back into it when the market improved. This is the kind of situation where a landlord may become flexible if he can be shown a real reason to do so.

At first, my client didn't want to show his company financials to the landlord, but I finally got him to agree. The landlord reviewed their books and told me that he couldn't give them any kind of relief because the principals in my client's company were taking out too much money. I had to agree with him, and went back to tell my client that they had to reduce their overhead, specifically the shareholders' salaries.

Ironically, they'd already done so, but hadn't shown those documents to me or to the landlord. My client simply updated the financials, and we were able to show the landlord that even with salary reductions, especially those of the shareholders, the monthly lease obligation was still putting an incredible burden on the company, preventing them from growing and getting back on their feet.

After reviewing the new documentation, the landlord agreed to give my client relief for four months by reducing the rent by more than half. However, he wanted a plan for repayment when the company could afford it. There was no reason for the landlord to be permanently out the money. In effect, my client received a short-term loan at no interest for eight months, and a ten-month repayment plan. This solution gave the client additional cash to build and market his business, and the landlord helped a tenant he wanted to keep. It worked out well for everyone.

Three months later, as it happened, I had to go back to the landlord and tell him that business had gotten even worse for my client. They really needed to get a smaller space from him, and pay the current market rates, with no payback when business got better. After several months of renegotiating, the landlord eventually did move the company into a new space, one that had been hard for him to lease at the current market rates. The company is now doing very well and they love their new space.

The key is to be creative, honest, and fair.

A Different Balance

Here is a different scenario: Your client's company is occupying space they *can* afford, but they really don't need it because they've consolidated their business. There are three years remaining on the lease and the rent is $10,000 per month, so the total present value of the lease is $360,000.

In these situations the landlord will often let a tenant get out for a specific amount of cash, *e.g.,* if the tenant pays up front about half the balance of the lease. But not all landlords will do this. Sometimes you have to convince the landlord that it's better to settle than to get into a fight—because then the tenant would simply stop paying.

Again, your approach will be critical. Some tenants would rather deal with a lawsuit than pay for useless space. Using our example, if the tenant pays about $180,000 or less from the total amount, this will give the landlord eighteen months to re-lease the space without losing any money. And if the landlord can lease it more quickly, the deal could be profitable for the landlord. On the other side, the tenant saves $180,000 (less whatever amount he pays for a new space).

In my client's case, the landlord didn't want to lose a tenant, but he also saw no reason to let them out of the lease. This is often true when times are hard and there's a lot of available space.

In such a situation you may need to get tough with the landlord. I told the landlord that my client was not going pay for unneeded space and was ready to stop paying and accept a lawsuit, *if necessary*. They would rather be forced out by a court after losing a lawsuit than continue to pay rent at the current rate. The landlord had to decide if it was worth going ahead with a lawsuit, or having twelve to eighteen months of rent, plus time to re-lease without losing money.

But note my *approach* to getting tough: I politely asked him if he really wanted to go through with a lawsuit. Wouldn't it be better to accept some money up front, with the possibility of leasing the space to someone else in the meantime? Always try and be nice and respectful during this phase. Don't show any anger or hostility; there is no need and it will almost certainly turn the tables against you.

You may wonder how it demonstrates integrity to threaten a landlord with non-payment that would result in a lawsuit. Hit the Refresh Button and consider the fact that the conditions when the client originally leased the space had changed significantly. When they signed the contract they had a booming business and needed the space. Now the space was useless for them and would soon be empty, or already was.

You may think that I am getting entangled in the "history" here. The point I want to make, however, is that conditions in the marketplace had changed. The landlord knew this and understood market conditions. Regardless of the original agreement, landlords must consider their tenants' needs, because empty spaces benefit no one. In this circumstance, money in the pocket is better than a signed lease. Unless a landlord wants to cut off his nose to spite his face, he will eventually agree to settle. (I use the masculine pronoun here because few women are this stupid. In my experience, women will almost always accept the settlement rather than create further conflict.)

More often than not, clients in such situations tell me that they have already offered this option to the landlord, and he has already rejected it. This doesn't deter me. I'm not the one who signed the lease in the first place, so the landlord is usually willing to be more open with me. I've learned how to speak to landlords and show them respect.

I've also learned how to listen, which is incredibly useful here. The landlord will tell you *why* he can't help you—if not directly, then indirectly—if you listen carefully. When I contact the landlord I often hear that the client has never really made a serious offer, or that the client has a bad attitude and doesn't really want to deal with the landlord. When I'm able to get a landlord to settle for half or less, my client is always surprised. More often than not, the client is surprised the landlord was even willing to speak to me.

2. Contract Renegotiations and Buyouts

Renegotiating contracts and buyouts is handled somewhat differently from simple real estate leases. In the introduction to this book, I mentioned a contract I'd renegotiated with Christine McKay's company. It was a typical situation in which Mypoints had signed up for something they now no longer needed, and had found another solution that was less expensive and more suitable.

In this case, we came up with a buyout solution for the contract that amounted to just under half the remaining cost of the contract, and this solution was agreeable to both parties. In this renegotiation I had used the sixth fundamental, *recognize attachments*, to appreciate what Christine was dealing with inside her company. Although this example was indeed similar to a lease buyout, the similarity was somewhat unusual.

The relationship between two sides won't always be smooth. Often one side (or both) will not have performed according to the contract, but doesn't want to admit it. Or there may be a disagreement regarding the performance of either side.

One of my clients had a number of problems with a service provider and wanted to get out of their contract. When I spoke to the service provider, they agreed there were problems, but felt that they were not in breach of the contract. The provider was correct in this particular instance, but my client was tired of dealing with problems with them and wanted out anyway.

This is a common scenario—one side wants to make good, but the other side has had enough and just wants out. What do you do? Hit the Refresh Button, because there is no apparent Solution to be found in the history.

Here the first fundamental, *understand the issues,* was an important ingredient in getting to a Solution. You have to move the renegotiation to a place where the other side (the provider in this example) can comprehend that, although they may have meant well, their execution was so poor that their customer (my client) simply cannot continue dealing with them.

You may, in fact, find that you have to be brutally honest. I often apologize for the situation and let the provider know that I've attempted to get my client to try again (which I always do) but to no avail. I explain that it's better for the provider to cut their losses and move on. They should spend their time with clients who appreciate their efforts, and build their business with new customers. I'm now in control of the Orange Ball, directing the renegotiation through respect for the provider's situation. They just need time to get used to the idea of losing a customer.

The harsh reality is that my client will no longer pay for the services. Though legally bound by the contract, my client has a good case based on the provider's poor performance. The provider company will often then blame their customer for lack of communication and point out other problems that have been caused by the customer. I explain that some companies are just not meant to do business together—there is no synergy. In the end, any contract should be about customer service. They eventually get the message and move on.

Money, Humor, and Credibility

Renegotiating a contract, or getting out of an existing one, often arises from customer service issues. When I was buying hundreds of thousands of plush toys in China, there were times when things

219

went wrong that were beyond our control. On one occasion I blew an order. It was late due to the tardy arrival of some components, and to make matters worse, part of the outfit was slightly off color.

The buyer was furious, but what could I do? The factory we used was usually very reliable, and they had produced the product as quickly as possible. Quite frankly, I hadn't noticed that the color was off. The buyer called up screaming, and I didn't know how to appease her.

What I said went something like this: "We have many customers and we know that sooner or later we're going to make mistakes. In an effort to be fair, we decided to put the names of all our customers in a hat and pick one at random." I told her we then focused all of our mistakes on this customer. "We pick a new customer each year," I told her. "And guess what? Your company got pulled from the hat for this year! We had no problems with any of our other customers. The good news is your name won't be in the hat next year."

I thought this was very humorous and rather cute and would help calm her down. But it was not that funny, or at all cute, and this was not the time or place—she was not amused. But when I told her I'd take care of the markdowns, and that we'd be much more careful with our quality control in the future, she did calm down somewhat. I promised her this would never happen again. *Be careful when using humor; it can backfire when not appropriate.*

The merchandise actually sold well so that my cost in dollars wasn't large—what I lost was credibility. *When money is not the issue, credibility is.* A company that has performed badly has to try like hell to regain and retain its credibility.

Today, I would handle that customer very differently. I would allow her to express her thoughts and anger, and then I would sincerely apologize. Hopefully, this would have gotten her to hit the Refresh Button. Unfortunately, in situations like this you really can't bring in a third party; you need to handle it directly. Since I created the problem, I had to fix it. Here I needed to apply fundamental two, *look for and create opportunities.*

It doesn't help to be cute when you get nervous. This is your chance to honestly admit your mistake and do the honorable thing by financially taking care of your customer, as well as making a personal commitment to do better in the future. The opportunities you find or create will give you credibility and will show that you understand the effect the problem is having on *your customer's* credibility.

You have to be aware that a situation like this affects your customer's credibility both within their own organization as well as with their customers. The fact that this company bought products from me, which my company shipped both late and incorrectly, reflects poorly on the buyer. This was very personal for the buyer, and because of that I had to assure her that I would take the blame within her company as well, which I did.

3. Contract Collections

Contract collections are different from what is usually thought of as "collections." I say this because these situations call for something more than just a bill collector. In a contract collection, a company or individual has signed a contract stating that they will pay a certain amount based on the performance of certain actions of another company or individual. The contract collection itself occurs when, for whatever reason, the company or individual has *decided* not to pay (not necessarily that they cannot *afford* to pay).

In contract collections, the seventh fundamental, *set the right goals,* is crucial. And you'll definitely need to get everyone to hit the Refresh Button. You'll also have to *transcend the details,* because how much is owed and how the debt was incurred are not important.

The Cavalry principle is also likely to be essential. If people or companies are not paying on a contract there is usually a good reason. Sometimes, though, it's difficult for the parties to deal directly with each other because of the history. Both would feel more open about discussing their issues with a third party. This also allows the emotional side to be discussed without fear of judgement.

A contract collection is the kind of issue that companies and individuals eventually hire lawyers to deal with, spending (wasting) thousands of dollars while everyone becomes more and more angry. I'm sorry to say that lawyers almost always make this kind of case worse. It's really not their fault; lawyers are trained to be advocates. But you'll never get control of the Orange Ball while everyone is angry or defensive. Using fundamentals one and six, *understand the issues* and *recognize attachments,* will generally work well in these situations.

There are several reasons why you're likely to hit the Refresh Button more than once. Companies (or individuals) who don't want to pay usually know that they're going to end up paying something. They know that some service was performed and something is due; they are simply refusing to pay the entire invoice. And the party who is owed the money usually knows they didn't perform to the level they should have.

The reasons don't matter. Both sides need to vent. Let them vent away, but eventually you have to get them both to understand that they will have to be realistic to resolve the matter. It's a waste of time to continue to fight. They need to agree on a fair amount to settle, and the Refresh Button may be their only chance.

I've represented both sides in this type of renegotiation and I handled them all the same way. At one time, I worked for a company that supposedly owed $80,000 to another company. We didn't think we owed anything, but to settle the matter we offered $2,500. This was after our respective lawyers had made a remarkable mess of things.

The lawyers on both sides made each other so angry that it became an ego war between the lawyers. I had heard that the judge himself was getting mad, and the issue was about to go to trial. I had a good relationship with the in-house counsel for our company, so I asked him if I could take a crack at it and call the owner of the other company directly to try and settle.

It was an interesting situation. The company we owed the money to had delivered a large amount of building materials to our building site. These materials were to be used not only for our office building project, but also for several other projects our contractor was building nearby. The contractor, who had placed the entire order under his company name, distributed the appropriate building materials to various construction sites, including ours.

As it happens, there is a surprising little law in Iowa which states that if the materials are delivered to your site, you're liable to pay for the entire lot—regardless of whom they're actually for. My company had already paid $17,000 to our contractor for the materials for our building, and we certainly didn't want to pay the entire balance of $63,000. But the contractor had left town—without paying *any* of the $80,000 invoiced for the materials. In other words, he kept our $17,000 and didn't pass any of it on to the company who had supplied the materials. (We had no idea if the contractor might also have been paid by his other customers.)

I called the owner of the building materials company, told him whom I represented, and informed him that I wasn't a lawyer. I opened the conversation by saying, "You must be really angry to find yourself in this predicament." He was indeed angry, and unloaded on me for fifteen minutes.

In accordance with the fifth fundamental, *find an approach and apply it,* while I merely listened and allowed him to vent, he managed to hit his own Refresh Button. This put the Orange Ball in my court. I told him that I understood the law, but I asked if he really thought it was fair that my company, after paying our portion in good faith to our contractor, should be liable for any part of the balance of the invoice?

I went on to furnish the owner with a copy of the cancelled check for our amount of the invoice, showing payment to the contractor. I also asked the owner if he was prepared to come to Iowa and spend a week in a courtroom to settle the situation. Even if he won, his lawyers' fees alone would be another $10,000.

I felt bad for him and offered him $2,000 to settle, so that everyone could move on to more interesting issues. He pointed out that our lawyer had offered him $2,500 a month ago. With a laugh, I told him that he should have taken it. He laughed, too, and agreed that both lawyers were creating more problems than they were worth.

In the end he settled for the $2,000 and was relieved to be through with the issue, thanking me for the way I handled it after the lawyers had spent four months on this whole discussion. I settled it in about two hours.

Why should we have paid *anything* to settle, since our part of the invoice had already been covered? We paid because we felt that the situation reflected poorly on our community and that the company should get something. Why was I able to quickly move the renegotiation to a Solution? Maybe it was like the top to a jar that comes off at a touch for one person, after someone else has struggled with it for many minutes. But I think it was simply that I was direct and honest, so the owner was able to settle down and think clearly. I also offered him a plausible argument that appealed to his sense of fairness.

4. Restructuring Debt:
Accounts Receivable/Accounts Payable

Many companies spend a great deal of money, and endure great embarrassment, by going bankrupt when they actually don't need to. The percentage of start-up companies that make it is not very high. We hear more about large companies, but it's usually the small, privately-held companies that go bankrupt.

There are two types of vendors to which a company owes money: secured vendors (the banks and other financial lenders) and unsecured vendors (everyone else). The secured vendors, seeking to gain control of a company, can usually force it into bankruptcy. In a bankruptcy, it's the secured vendors who usually get control of the Orange Ball (along with most of the money). These large debtors are taken care of first. Even the bankruptcy lawyers are paid first.

What money is left is divided among the unsecured debtors. In reality, this means that virtually nothing is left for the smaller vendors. In my opinion, this is not right. Your company will be much better off if you can renegotiate your debt so that *the vendors who have really served you are paid first;* then you just close your doors, rather than going bankrupt. However, this is not always possible.

In for a Penny

A very large company I had sold merchandise to owed me $45,000. They filed for Chapter 11, a form of bankruptcy that allows a company to restructure its secured debt. In this situation, unsecured debtors get very little. After two years, I received about $2,000 and 25 shares of stock.

The company restructured and got out of bankruptcy, and is doing fine today. At the stock's highest point, the 25 shares were worth $1,800. I received about $1,500 when I sold them. Later, I found out that the bankruptcy lawyers had been paid ten million dollars.

It happens every day. Unfortunately, none of my principles or fundamentals could have helped me get more money. I had to hit the Refresh Button and move on. Years later, I did have the opportunity to sell to this company again and make money on future orders.

Cash Flow Crunch

Here's a common scenario: Companies find themselves in a cash flow crunch because their revenue can't cover their monthly obligations, and they have no other resources for additional funding. If your company finds itself in this situation, my suggestion is to re-figure your payables using the following formula:

> *The amount you can afford to spend*
> *each month should be about ten percent*
> *less than your monthly revenue.*

For instance, if your monthly revenue is $100,000 and your monthly payables are $300,000, you'll have to *renegotiate* your payables, plus your overhead, so that together, they total no more than $90,000 per month. But you can't rely solely on reducing your payables. You must also look at your fixed expenses: rent, salaries, etc. Then you must figure out how to get your revenues up to at least $300,000.

A company that is short of cash usually stops paying its vendors. Vendors who scream loudly enough and threaten to cut off services will get paid first—the squeaky wheel really does get the grease. As a result, there will be little or no money left for the other vendors. To my way of thinking, however, it's much better to pay something to every vendor.

To do this, the company must renegotiate its payables. How? Be up-front with the vendors. This is the time to be proactive and take control of the Orange Ball. Fundamental number seven, *set the right goals,* can help preserve your integrity and credibility.

Don't wait until your payments are late, or until the vendor calls you. It shows a great deal of respect to the vendor when *you* call first to let them know you can't pay their invoice in full. Then, once you have set your goals, you'll know what you can afford to pay each vendor. When you call to arrange a payment plan without an interruption of services, the vendor will often lend a helping hand. Vendors, naturally, prefer honest customers who ask for help, rather than those who abruptly stop paying altogether. This approach affords you the preferable option of paying every vendor at least something.

The first thing is to separate your short-term debt from your long-term debt, the latter being more difficult (though usually not impossible) to reduce. The vendors you work with every day will usually cooperate and continue to serve you as long as you either pay cash for any new merchandise or remain current with any new invoices. Eventually, however, your vendors will want to know exactly what's going on. Call them regularly and keep them up to date; don't wait for them to call you. Later on, once you've created a payment plan and demonstrated your ability to stick to it, you won't have to keep calling the vendors.

You'll need to deal differently with vendors who are on a monthly payment plan, and those to whom you owe a fixed amount. This is the time to be persistent. Such situations frequently involve a contract, an agreement for equipment, or a bank loan. Leases are difficult to deal with, but the companies will deal if you give them a good reason to do so. *A company will take less if they know that whatever they can get is the best figure they're ever going to get.*

Generally speaking, leasing companies and banks will work with you and let you pay less per month for a short period of time. But be careful. Banks will often cut their losses early. If you go to a bank and tell them you can't pay them back on time, they could call the loan and put you out of business. Your bank will request financial statements, and if your statements show that you're not solvent, they could very well pull the loan. Before requesting a new payment plan, try to get a sense of which way the bank may respond. It's critical to come in with a solid plan of how you're going to pay back the bank.

Here's a piece of important advice: *only sign a contract or lease on behalf of a company.* Never sign it personally, even if the company demands that you do so. When you sign, put your title next to your name to indicate that you are signing on the company's behalf. This ensures that you can't be held personally responsible for payments, no matter what happens to the company in the future.

Renegotiating the amount owed to equipment leasing companies is a long process: be patient. These are large companies and they're not flexible. Even if you return the equipment, you still may be liable for the balance due (which is another good reason never to personally sign a lease).

It's often possible to renegotiate your monthly payments to a leasing company down to the lowest amount you can afford. You have to be honest and steadfast, but you must also be careful. If a company senses that you might not pay them, they could put you into involuntary bankruptcy. Usually, three vendors have to get together and petition the court to place you into involuntary bankruptcy. Therefore it's important never to let any of your vendors know who your other vendors are.

I worked with a company that was more than $140 million in debt. The company had about eight million in cash, and around $50,000 in monthly revenue. Cash flow wasn't the issue to cover their short-term monthly nut; the enormous debt was their concern.

I renegotiated the debt down to around three million, and settled with each vendor on an individual basis. Some were told they would get nothing, others got a little, and with others we demanded back all or part of our deposits. We received over one million in returned deposits, and paid off about $1.8 million to get out of the other contracts. Those who deserved to get some money settled

229

with us and were very satisfied, and those who didn't deserve anything ended up receiving nothing.

Many of these contracts had originally been negotiated and signed by an executive team who didn't have the best interests of the company at heart and were eventually fired. Actually, many of our vendors understood that they were not entitled to receive their full invoice, if anything, which is why so many deposits were returned to us. By using these principles, the company never filed for bankruptcy, settled its debts, and saved everyone time, money, and reputation.

When a company is basically healthy and has great potential, you can restructure the debt by renegotiating monthly obligations so that the company can preserve its cash. They can build a cash reserve at the same time they're building their revenue stream, and ultimately get their finances back into the black.

---

5. Personal Contracts

From the perspective of renegotiating, personal contracts are essentially the same as professional ones, except that they tend to involve a lot more emotion. Given that there is usually more history in personal contracts, commitments, and agreements, the fifth fundamental, *find an approach and apply it*, is especially important.

It's very important to consider how you'll approach those you care about most, particularly when you need to break, or have already broken, a promise or commitment; the same is true when someone has broken a promise or commitment to you. I cannot emphasize enough the importance of hitting the Refresh Button and then just *listening*. You need to show those you care about, and who care about you, at least as much respect as anyone else you have dealings with. Most importantly in these situations, don't take the other person for granted. Be honest, kind, and nice. And by all means, listen to each other. Really listen. Be silent and don't interrupt. Remember to *behave as if it is personal and react as if it is business.*

Most personal contracts are oral, not written, but they still need to be renegotiated from time to time as circumstances change.

You may say personal agreements aren't really contracts or renegotiations: I contend that they are. *They're the commitments and promises we make to one another.* And they're usually with the people about whom we care the most—our children, spouses, parents, siblings, and good friends, all of whom deserve our utmost respect and care.

Many of us are more casual about personal contracts because they're not usually about money, and involve people and relationships we may take for granted. This is a mistake. I'm not a psychologist, but I promise you that if you use the techniques and principles in this book in your personal life, you'll have much better relationships, at work and at home, especially with those who are closest to you.

Once you begin thinking in terms of renegotiating, it becomes apparent that we need to renegotiate personal promises and agreements more often than one might suppose. Why? Because everyone changes and grows. It's natural that we'll need and want different things at different times. Again, the Refresh Button principle is a vital component in personal renegotiations. Because emotions can run high, it's always important to get those involved to sit quietly and listen to each other.

The Oldest Agreement

The most renegotiated contract in the world is the marriage contract. The verbal and emotional experience at the beginning of the relationship will change over time. It's a much-touted fact that fifty percent of all marriages in the U.S. end up in divorce. Why? Usually it's because of the unwillingness of one or both parties to renegotiate the relationship.

The implicit terms of the initial agreement continually change as the parties get older, as finances change for better or worse, as children become part of the equation, and later when children leave home. All of these factors inevitably change the needs and desires of both parties.

I've been married to the same wonderful woman for 32 years and it's the best deal I ever made. Yet no matter how committed we were to each other 32 years ago, our relationship has been renegotiated many times. Not because we're in the habit of breaking our promises—quite the contrary. It's just that life is full of changes.

We raised three wonderful children, my wife earned her Ph.D., and I've had a variety of jobs. My wife is a very self-sufficient individual and likes her time alone. Until recently, this meant that apart from helping out with the kids, I could organize my time to suit myself. For me, this was a fantastic arrangement.

Now we are "empty nesters," and all of a sudden she's looking to me for companionship. It's a renegotiation of our relationship. Because I love my wife and want to keep our marriage strong, I'm working on fulfilling her new needs. I may not be there one hundred percent of the time, but I'm getting better. I do enjoy our time together, so this renegotiation is quite rewarding for me. Unfortunately, we sometimes define "together time" differently.

The Grandmother Factor

The most dominating negotiator, or renegotiator, I've ever known was my grandmother. Actually, there are many people who had a grandmother like mine. Born in Eastern Europe and brought to the U.S. at a young age, she lived through the big San Francisco earthquake and the Depression.

Before it was decided about twenty years ago that win-win negotiations are both possible and preferable, most people negotiated like my grandmother. They wanted to win at all cost. They wanted to make the best deal for themselves, whether or not it was good for the other side. And they used guilt and bribery to get what they wanted, disregarding the feelings of others. Don't get me wrong, I loved and adored my Grandmother.

Whenever we went to her house for a meal, we all knew that in the end, no one could win her favor. And by the time we left the house, we all felt that we owed her something, no matter what we had done. She would fill our plates with food: roast beef, mashed potatoes, vegetables, and sometimes, a second kind of meat as well. (This was after the matzo ball chicken soup and chopped liver.)

There would be fifteen people at the table and she kept an accounting in her head of exactly what, and how much, each person was eating. If we didn't choose a particular dish, or didn't finish one, she would ask what was wrong with it. Being full was no excuse. She would come around with seconds on everything, starting with the soup. If you didn't want seconds, you'd hear the line we all dreaded: "I have no use for you."

Later in his life, my Uncle Sandy (her son) and his wife Aunt Helen, used this line so much that their friends now use it among themselves as a joke. But I can tell you that when my grandmother used it, it was no joke. It was a deal-closer on any deal. My grandmother said it with a straight face and with conviction, and whether you were five years old or sixty, you knew that she owned you. She controlled the Orange Ball. "I have no use for you" was an A-bomb to self-esteem. Boom! Hardly a scrap left. Anyone with that degree of power over another person has won before the first word is spoken—but at what cost?

In her later years, we laughed with her about it. But still, whenever she wanted something from you, or wanted you to do something and you didn't do it, the dreaded line would be uttered. It wasn't even necessary to engage her very much to trigger it. She might make a conversational remark, or ask you a question, and if your immediate response wasn't to her liking, you got it. In order to just get along with my grandmother and keep peace in the family, we would all constantly hit the Refresh Button without even knowing it.

Most people today don't negotiate or renegotiate the way my grandmother did. It's now pretty well established that this approach doesn't work in the long run, because it creates poor working relationships and hinders success. And life is nothing if not one big, long run. I love the old saying, "What goes around, come around."

Another experience with my grandmother taught me a great deal. My parents were out of town and my grandmother, who hated hospitals and distrusted doctors, had to go into the hospital. Uncle Sandy was trying to take care of her there, but no matter what he did, her response was, "I have no use for you."

When I arrived at the hospital, she'd already been there for a week and my uncle was utterly frustrated. I met him as I came out of the elevator. He threw his arms in the air.

"You take care of her," he yelled. "I've tried, and she's impossible!"

My grandmother was 87 at the time, mentally clear, and feisty as ever. When I entered her room she immediately told me that she wanted to go home. (The nurse had already informed me that the doctor wouldn't release her.)

"Grandma," I said, "this is America. It's a free country and you're not in jail. If you want to go home, get dressed and I'll take you home."

"But the nurse said I can't do that."

Now, you don't say "can't" in our family—we take it as a personal challenge and immediately try to get around whatever someone is saying we can't do. Even if it's something we don't particularly want, the challenge is on.

"Why not?" I said. "What's the worst that could happen?" Here I took control of the Orange Ball.

I spoke to the nurse again, and she said she couldn't guarantee my grandmother would live much longer if she went home early.

"She's 87," I told the nurse. "She's going to die sometime."

Then I turned to my grandmother, "The nurse is worried that if you go home you may die. Do you still want to go home?"

"I don't care. They're trying to kill me here."

I said to the nurse, "There's your answer. Get her dressed and I'll take her home."

I signed some papers and took my grandmother home. That was the one day when she didn't say that she had no use for me. It felt great, as if I'd finally won a deal with her—even though later at her house, when I didn't do something she wanted quickly enough, again she had no use for me. I just looked at her and she smiled the greatest, most mischievous smile. To this day I miss her.

What I take from this particular experience is that we have to be aware of the consequences of our actions. Whether negotiating or renegotiating, keep in mind how your words and actions will affect the other party. If you can do this, you'll have a great deal of control over the process and the outcome.

A California-based internet company, Cybergold, used to sell advertising on the net. Their slogan was *"Pay attention, attention pays."* I loved that slogan: it's true in everything we do. We're all either negotiating or renegotiating something all the time; we're just not always aware of it. We're also constantly witnessing other people negotiating or renegotiating. We only have to pay attention.

It's worth paying attention to what's going on around you so you can draw upon these experiences later. I remember seeing an interview with an actor who was asked if he ever made use of his real life experiences while acting.

He described a time when he was in the middle of a heated argument with his wife. He was very angry, but all of a sudden he stopped and thought: "If I can remember this feeling, the tone of my voice"—he said he even looked in the mirror to see the expression on his face—"then I could use this state of mind in some appropriate scene." He wanted to remember every single thing about the emotion he was experiencing so that he could use it in his profession. Probably not the best thing to do for the relationship with his wife, but nevertheless he *was* paying attention to a particular experience.

Favor for a Friend

I had an embarrassing experience the other day. My wife and I are the godparents of three boys who live in California. I've always been very close to them and I'd especially wanted one of them (let's call him Peter) to come to a visitor's weekend at the university campus where I live—with a view to his attending in the fall. For a variety of reasons I believe this university would be an ideal school for him. It took me a long time to convince both him and his parents to come for one of the weekends.

A very good friend (we'll call her Emma) and her husband have also been close to Peter's parents for many years. Ever since Peter was in grade school, Emma and her husband, who is a professor and trustee of the university, have also thought it would be wonderful if one or more of the kids might attend here, especially Peter. Over the years, they too have spent hours talking to Peter's parents about this.

Emma's daughter is an admissions counselor at the university, so I asked her if Peter should stay on campus for the visitor's weekend in April, and she said yes. Emma was delighted that I had finally managed to convince the parents and Peter to at least come to town for a visitor's weekend, and she complimented me on my achievement and expressed appreciation for my fulfilling my role as godfather.

A few days later she called to say she'd been thinking about inviting Peter to stay with them. It seemed to her an ideal arrangement.

Without thinking, I told her (rather abruptly) that we'd already decided he would be better off staying in campus housing among the other students.

Emma pointed out that Peter wouldn't be with other students, but would be housed with the other weekend guests.

I became loud and huffy and said that if he wasn't going to stay with students on campus, he should stay with us. After a few minutes listening to my ranting, she said that she had to hang up, and she did.

I realized I'd upset her, but I was also upset with her. I thought, what audacity to invite Peter without even asking me. From my point of view, I had every right to be upset. But I also realized I might have hurt one of my very best friends with my negative response.

First, I had to hit the Refresh Button. I had to get over being upset with her to begin to understand what just took place. Even knowing someone well doesn't guarantee you can predict their reactions. Obviously, she hadn't predicted my response to her phone call. And I hadn't thought about why she did what she did and what her intentions were. I sent a brief apologetic e-mail, thinking that would do it—my second mistake.

Knowing Emma, I should have realized that it was a big deal for her to invite a teenage boy into her home. Her intentions were pure, to be warmly hospitable and offer Peter an opportunity to be with her daughter to talk more casually about going to this particular university. She would never dream of usurping my position as godfather, or in any way minimize the efforts I had made to arrange

Peter's visit. As a friend, she was shocked by my response, and her feelings were hurt.

If I had really listened to what Emma was telling me, taking into account who she really was, we could have had an intelligent, coherent discussion of what might be best for Peter.

If I had acknowledged her offer and thanked her for making it, I could have easily suggested we get together and plan the best possible experience for Peter.

Instead, I jumped to conclusions and let my ego direct the interaction, without even considering the variety of alternatives and variations on our respective plans for Peter's visit.

The point of this tale is that once you hurt someone's feelings, *nothing else matters*. You can't try and discuss the issues to make it better. The solution, as the fourth principle states, is never in the details.

You must address the emotional damage caused by bad behavior or it will be very difficult to reach a solution. You have to acknowledge what you've done. Bottom line—try to never respond impulsively. If you attempt to create a solution and try to settle the issue, *without* owning up to your bad behavior and taking responsibility for the damage it caused on the feeling level, you'll have an empty settlement, if any settlement at all. There will continue to be a not-quite-right feeling between the parties, which will only hurt the relationship (or the deal), and may even contribute to its destruction.

Taking full responsibility for your behavior towards other people, and its impact on their feelings, is particularly important in personal relationships, because *you must continue to interact with each other.* The longer you put it off, the more emotional baggage you accrue. It's better to deal with these situations as soon as possible and not put them off.

The next morning I went to Emma's house to apologize, making my third mistake: I tried to explain and defend my actions. I didn't address my *behavior,* but instead tried to spin my apology by presenting a set of *reasons.* As soon as I walked in I could see that she was upset. I gave her a hug and said I was really sorry.

She pushed me away and burst into tears. "You can't just *say* you're sorry," she said. "Those are just words. I'm editing your book every day, reading all your stories about how 'behavior counts' and then you treat me as if I'm not even your friend." That comment hit home.

Whenever you hurt someone's feelings (especially when they are really trying to reach out and do something nice, as Emma was) nothing else matters. You have to give emotionally to the point where their hurt is soothed, and this takes more than "I'm sorry." They *are* just words: you have to deal with the emotions involved. Your apology should also acknowledge the good intentions of the person you hurt.

Also, when you react impulsively towards another person, you really aren't listening to what they are saying. Therefore, you're showing them no respect. When you're close to people, it seems as if it's OK to say anything, but that's often when you say something or do something thoughtless, and in a split second you've hurt the person and the relationship.

We often act impulsively with those we love the most. In this case, I should have just stopped, listened, and asked her why she thought it was better for Peter to stay with her, and let her explain herself.

Then I could have said, "Can we think about this before you call his mother?" I should not have responded by yelling, "No way!"

Impulsive reactions almost always cause trouble. Now I get that Emma felt she was doing a great thing by welcoming Peter to her home. We've made up and all is well, but what a great lesson it was. I needed to hit the Refresh Button for myself, prior to reacting to Emma's call. I should have used the fifth fundamental, *find an approach and apply it,* prior to e-mailing her *and* before going over the next day to make peace. I also should have used the first fundamental, *understand the issues,* prior to responding at all. If I'd applied my own principles, the whole interaction would have proceeded very differently.

The Refresh Button principle is an amazing tool. And the techniques of *listening, being nice,* and *using humor* to help hit the Refresh Button work very well. These techniques have helped me tremendously in both my personal and professional life. They insure that my intentions are honest, and they force me to behave as I should—in a respectful and pleasant manner. But as you can see, it requires constant vigilance to put your best face forward.

These techniques will help you, too. They help to get control of the Orange Ball, and to get it back when you've lost it. Don't mistake the Refresh Button for being weak or complacent. It's a powerful tool that will help lower the emotional temperature and give a proper direction to the renegotiation process. The Refresh Button allows everyone to focus on the ultimate goal.

Applying the proper principle and using the fundamentals at the appropriate time will enable you to move any renegotiation forward more quickly. All the different types of renegotiations we discussed in this chapter create an opportunity for us to behave properly in sometimes very difficult situations.

Conclusion

In the United States we've been brought up to believe that *all men are created equal.* And in the eyes of God, I believe this is true. But in the eyes of man, we're not. I don't mean this in an elitist or bigoted sense: there are basic differences between people. Some of us are tall, some short, some thin, and some (like myself) could stand to shed a few pounds. Some people are delicate physically while others always seem to be heartier. If we consider the mental side of life, we find that certain people just seem to be smarter than others. Some are street smart and some are academically smart, and few are both.

We all have strengths and weaknesses, but no matter how we differ from one another, we must learn to treat each other with respect. *In any renegotiation, nothing matters more than giving respect to the people you're dealing with. You'll reap the rewards of this for a long time to come.*

In the appendices at the end of this book, you'll find a workbook to use when progressing through a renegotiation. I've also listed some books on negotiation (and life) that you might find valuable, and a few web sites you might find interesting as further resources.

You should now understand my position on *Renegotiating with Integrity.* I hope you can believe me when I say that you're much more powerful than you give yourself credit for, and you affect the people you deal with. And remember, *it's not business, it's personal!*

Recommended Reading

The following books have been most useful in my own work and often prove valuable to those who are starting out in the practice of renegotiation. They're presented in order of specific relevance to renegotiating, but all of them are valuable additions to any business library.

You Can Negotiate Anything — Herb Cohen (Bantam, 1982) ISBN 0553281097.

"The Power of Nice: How to Negotiate So Everyone Wins—Especially You!" — Ronald M. Shapiro and Mark A. Jankowski (Wiley, 2001) ISBN 0471080721.

"Bullies, Tyrants, and Impossible People: How to Beat Them Without Joining Them" — Ronald M. Shapiro and Mark A. Jankowski (Crown Business, 2005) ISBN 1400050111.

Negotiate This!: By Caring, But Not T-H-A-T Much — Herb Cohen (Warner, 2006) ISBN 0446696447.

Getting to Yes — Roger Fisher, William L. Ury, and Bruce Patton (Random House, 2003) ISBN 1844131467.

Negotiating Skills for Managers — Steven P. Cohen (McGraw-Hill, 2002) ISBN 0071387579.

The Art of the Deal — Donald J. Trump with Tony Schwartz (Random House, 1987) ISBN 0394555287.

The Science of Getting Rich or Financial Success Through Creative Thought — Wallace D. Wattles (Iceni Books, 2002) ISBN 1587360942.

The Essential Guide to Increasing Small Business Profitability — John D. Viviano (Rishi Publishing, 2002) ISBN 0972149201.

The Intelligent Negotiator: What to Say, What to Do, How to Get What You Want – Every Time — Charles Craver (Three Rivers Press, 2002) ISBN 1400081491.

TM – Transcendental Meditation: A New Introduction to Maharishi's Easy, Effective and Scientifically Proven Technique for Promoting Better Health, Unfolding Your Creative Potential, and Creating Peace in the World — Robert Roth (Plume, 1994) ISBN 1556114036.

Contented Cows Give Better Milk — Bill Catlette and Richard Hadden (Williford Communications, 2000) ISBN 1890651109.

APPENDIX B

Workbook

The following pages are extracted from Marc's renegotiation workshops. Feel free to copy these pages and use them for your own renegotiation planning and execution. Although they are copyrighted by Marc, you are given express permission to reproduce them for personal use in the renegotiation process.

For more information on Marc Freeman workshops and seminars, or to obtain permission for non-personal reproduction of these pages, please visit www.MarcFreeman.us.

Prior to Any Renegotiation,
Review the Renegotiation Checklist

Preparation (before you begin)

1. Identify the potential agreement or relationship that needs to be renegotiated.

2. Decide if it is worth the time and effort to proceed.

3. Decide who is best equipped to do the renegotiating.

4. Create an end goal — your comfort zone — and be flexible with it.

5. Understand the history of the parties involved.

Action (after the process has begun)

6. Listen to the other side's perspective and see where it matches or doesn't match the reality of your position.

7. After hearing their position, create a plan to get to a Common Ground.

8. Ask the other side what they see as a Plausible Solution.

9. If you cannot accept their Solution, begin to present your side.

10. Work with the other side to create a Solution, and the common Comfort Zone will emerge. From there, the settlement is usually simple.

If you don't answer these questions first, you'll enter the renegotiation blind.

_____

_____

_____

_____

_____

It's Not Business, It's Personal

It's Personal for Both Sides

- Your behavior creates your reputation.

- The effect is personal for those with whom you renegotiate.

Behave as if it is Personal
React as if it is Business

_____

_____

_____

_____

_____

_____

_____

_____

_____

_____

_____

_____

Freeman's Five Principles of Successful Renegotiation

1. The Critical Path
2. The Secret of the Orange Ball
3. Hit the Refresh Button
4. Transcend the Details
5. Call in the Cavalry

_____

_____

_____

_____

_____

_____

_____

_____

_____

_____

_____

_____

_____

The Critical Path Principle

You must follow the Critical Path to renegotiate successfully

Four Landmarks for Any Successful Renegotiation

1. Common Ground
2. Plausible Solution
3. Comfort Zone
4. Settlement

_____

_____

_____

_____

_____

_____

_____

_____

_____

_____

What You May Find Along the Critical Path

The Settlement Is Not Always Fair

It's important not to get attached.

Being right is not always the issue.

Find the Right Person

Who is the decision maker?

Filter the decision.

Move up the corporate ladder.

When Someone Keeps Saying "NO"

How many NO's can you take?

Get creative; look for out-of-the-box approaches.

Ask a lot of questions.

Giving In Is Not a Sign of Weakness

Learn how to move on.

Know When Not to Get Involved

_____

_____

_____

_____

The Orange Ball Principle

You must know who's in control of the Orange Ball,
and how to get it back,
to renegotiate successfully.

- What is Winning?

- Behave Properly

- Becoming Attached

- Playing Good Cop and Bad Cop

- How to Tell Who is in Control of the Orange Ball

- How to get Control of the Orange Ball

- Avoid Renegotiating with Yourself

_____

_____

_____

_____

_____

_____

_____

_____

The Refresh Button Principle

You must never overreact or act impulsively
— take a deep breath and listen.

Importance of the Right Approach

Three Techniques:

- Listen
- Be Nice
- Use Humor

_____

_____

_____

_____

_____

_____

_____

_____

_____

_____

The Transcending Principle

You must go beyond the details
in order to stay on the Critical Path.

Where to Find a Solution

The Solution is not always in the details.

How much of the final solution will involve the details of the original contract, deal, or agreement? (It's rarely about money alone.)

Lawyers generally don't make good renegotiators.

_____

_____

_____

_____

_____

_____

_____

_____

_____

_____

The Seven Fundamentals of Renegotiating

1. Understand the Issues
2. Look for Opportunities
3. Find a Reason
4. Stay Honest
5. Find an Approach and Apply It
6. Recognize Attachments
7. Get the Goals Right

_____

_____

_____

_____

_____

_____

_____

_____

_____

_____

_____

_____

The Cavalry Principle

Make sure you have the right person
renegotiating at all times.
If not, call in the cavalry.

Know When to Bring in a Third Party:

- You need to get the egos out of the way.

- The players are too emotionally involved.

- The other party refuses to speak to you.

- You need to settle prior to the trial.

_____

_____

_____

_____

_____

_____

_____

_____

_____

Different types of Renegotiating
Applying the Principles

- Contract Renegotiations

- Contract Buyouts

- Contract Collection

- Real Estate Lease Renegotiations

- Real Estate Lease Buyouts

- Restructuring Debt (Accounts Payables / Receivables)

- Personal Contracts

During your Next Renegotiating Opportunity
Ask yourself the Following Questions:

What are the main reasons for renegotiating?

_____

_____

What changes took place that created an opportunity to renegotiate?

_____

_____

Will it be necessary for someone to hit the Refresh Button and why?

_____

_____

Will you know who's in control of the Orange Ball?

_____

_____

Is the right person renegotiating for you?

_____

_____

APPENDICES

APPENDIX C

About the Author

Bringing integrity to renegotiating is Marc Freeman's passion. He renegotiates hundreds of millions of dollars in contracts all over the world. A recognized expert in his field, Marc has developed a unique, practical approach to renegotiating—*renegotiating with integrity*—based on the simple but profound principles of respect, honesty, creativity, and clear communication.

Marc gives frequent workshops and presentations on *Renegotiating with Integrity*. He customizes his *Renegotiating Skills* programs to meet the specific needs of executives and managers, sales people, customer service associates, and human resource managers. An extraordinarily powerful, interesting, and humorous speaker, Marc is often requested to give his unique presentation on *Renegotiating Your Happiness*.

For more than a decade, Marc has been a consultant on strategy, sales and marketing, product development, product sourcing, and importing. After renegotiating more than $100,000,000 in contracts for USA Global Link, he created Marc Freeman & Associates in 2001, specializing in renegotiating contracts and consult-

259

ing. Drawing upon his 30 years of experience as an entrepreneur, Marc also provides management training, executive coaching, and CEO mentoring.

Speaking and giving workshops around the world give Marc the opportunity to let people know that behavior counts, and that success in personal and professional life is achieved on this basis. Marc's message is simple: "It's not business, it's personal."

More about Marc's Experience and Credentials

Born and raised in San Francisco, Marc has been happily married for 32 years; with three grown children, he now resides in Fairfield, Iowa. Marc has a degree in Architecture from the University of California, Berkeley. He is also a teacher of the Transcendental Meditation Program™.

In 1978 Marc was promoted to VP of National Sales and Import Manager for Coffee Imports International, and in 1984 moved to Fairfield, where he became president and owner of Super Radiance Art Glass, and a president and partner in Franland. In 1988 he merged the two successful companies into Tarsha International, which became the largest supplier of plush toys to upscale department stores for Easter and Christmas theme programs.

In 1990, Marc started Polardreams International, and with a new partner, opened a factory in China to produce bath and stationary gift sets for major membership clubs, including Sam's, Costco, and BJ's, also selling to Wal-Mart, Marshall's, and TJ Maxx. In 1998, Marc sold his share of Polardreams International and became the President of Special Operations and head of Sales and Marketing for USA Global Link.

Acknowledgements

I must first acknowledge Marci, my wife; she is one of the most moral people I know and has taught me a great deal about who I should be as a human being. I also must thank her for all the work and dedication she put into proofreading and indexing this book. She has also honed my renegotiation skills over the past 32 years by giving me lots of practice.

I could not write this without acknowledging the input of the three greatest accomplishments of my life, Jonathan, Leela, and Eliana. I feel I can now go to each of them for advice, which I often do.

My parents would be so proud of my having written a book, especially since they know I haven't read many. They would be amazed.

My brother, Rabbi Gordon Freeman has been a moral compass for me as long as I can remember. He has constantly shown me, by his own example, how to be a better father, husband, and human being.

I have to thank my brother Gary for teaching me what it means to be a real friend and that loyalty is important.

I want to remember my Grandma Rose for all she gave me, but especially for the unconditional love that I know she felt for me even when she had no use for me.

Thanks also go to my Uncle Sanford, who told me it was OK to go to Israel after high school and not go directly to college. That trip changed my life and set in motion a chain of events that is why I am here today. And to Aunt Helen for just being the best: so understanding and loving that she inspires everyone in the family how to behave with graciousness, integrity, and love.

Dr. Robert Keith Wallace and Samantha Wallace gave me the idea to write this book, and the confidence that I *could* write it, from the very first chapter. Samantha spent hours editing, and teaching me *my own lessons* by showing me the importance of what I was writing about. She is a true friend and I love her for her help and support. Keith's wisdom has always been an inspiration to me.

The wisdom of Dr. Christopher Hartnett, and his understanding of my skills, have been invaluable. I am especially indebted to him for the Orange Ball and Refresh Button principles. He and his wife Linda have given me constant and unwavering support and friendship.

Nat and Marilyn Goldhaber have been great supporters in so many ways that I will be grateful to them forever. Nat has constantly recognized my skills and found opportunities for me to use them.

My deepest gratitude goes to Herb Cohen for his generosity in writing the Foreword to this book. He has been gracious to me from the moment I met him. As far as I am concerned, Herb is the father of modern negotiation techniques and led the way with enormous integrity and character. Herb Cohen is a *mensch*.

Warren and Harriet Berman have always been there when I needed help and encouragement.

Toby and Charley Lieb have also been very good friends, over so many years. Charlie, who has since passed, supported me in every business I've ever had. He was so balanced in his view of business

262

and life that I could always count on him to give me an honest, mature, moral, and enlightened perspective on any issue. Toby is a great friend and confidant.

Len and Dena Oppenheim have constantly supported my efforts to succeed. Len's insightful advice about this book was very much appreciated.

Margaret and Rashi Glazer have given me so much support and encouragement. Rashi, a Marketing Professor at the UC Berkeley Haas School of Business, guided the visual look and feel of this book.

Thanks to Bonnie Barnett, who spent hours helping edit this book. Through many changes, she constantly praised the book and gave me the confidence to continue.

When I told Samantha that Allen Cobb was going to do the final edit and layout, she laughed and said, "And you think I'm picky; you haven't seen anything yet." In my opinion, Allen took this book from great to greater.

John and Lynn Lass have been good friends. John has often promoted my renegotiating skills.

Thanks to Brenda and John Narducci for guiding Josie Hannes in the work she did for me.

Many thanks to Josie, who designed the cover of this book and all of my graphics, including the Orange Ball logo.

Barry Pitt has given me the opportunity to test out my theories on more than one occasion. His wife Jane is a good friend and a great supporter.

Thanks also go to Lee Moczygemba, of American Training, who has taught me how to speak professionally, and has been a constant supporter. She has also helped to make all of my materials (including this book) more professional on every level. Thanks to Jim Bagnola for introducing me to this most wonderful woman.

Tina and Peter Sterling have been unbelievably supportive. Tina's brilliant insights enabled me to bring out more clearly what I was trying to say.

Bill Volkman, my first boss, taught me so much about how to sell, product development, and importing. He also taught me how to enjoy life. He has been wonderfully supportive of my career and is a true friend.

Bill Zimmerman taught me not to be attached to any deal and always hire someone smarter that you are. He was a wonderful friend and advisor and I miss him very much.

Arjuna Matlin grew up with my son and became a great friend and supporter. I am so proud of his success on all levels.

David and Joan Scheiner for always being there for me. They have inspired me to be better. I love them dearly.

Francesca Hoerlein, my first business partner, taught me good design and style and personal morality.

Alan Unger was a great partner, and we created some great "top ten" stories together (some of which are in this book).

John Viviano has been so gracious with his time and experience, has encouraged me to keep going, and has kept me on the right track.

Tim and Eliza Mar taught me that always striving to be the best and deliver the best is a worthy cause and a real discipline toward keeping your integrity. They have done just that with *Chefshop.com*, the best food site on the net.

Bob Wright of the Wright Learning Institute in fifteen minutes got me off my rear and told me to start marketing myself. I have been motivated to succeed every day since that conversation.

Christine McKay, as a great renegotiator herself, continually offers encouragement, friendship, and advice.

Richard and Cissy Swig for inspiring and mentoring me when I was just getting started in my business career. They were both generous and supportive.

I want to remember Ken Ketterhagen, who was my good friend and lawyer. He left us much too early and I miss him greatly.

Finally, I need to thank His Holiness Maharishi Mahesh Yogi for giving me the greatest knowledge of life. Also, for creating Fairfield, the greatest community in the world—with the most creative and dynamic people.

Here's a list of people who are no less important, but I'm running out of space. I put them in alphabetical order because no one is more or less important than another:

David Addelson, Elka Altbach, Janet Atwood, John Baker of *Negotiator Magazine,* Alan Balmer, Jesse Berkowitz, Julie and Steve Blum, Sal Bonavita, Debbie Brill, Melanie Brown, Steve Brown of Crocodile Creek, Mr. Bert Callen and Mrs. Danise Chandler (my high school English teachers), Sandy and Stan Crowe, Clyde Cleveland, Kyle Cleveland, Steven P. Cohen, Stan Deck, Lynda and

Michael Dimmik, Dean Draznin, Monique and Matthew Epstein, Gillian and Stephen Foster, Ken Glattfelder and the gang at Ottumwa Printing, Michael Goodman, Richard Hadden, Tim Hawthorne, Lonica Halley, Steve Kaston, Steve Juskewycz, Len Labagh, David Landis, Craig Lawson, Eileen and Alan Leeds, Marc Linden, Greg Lowenberg and all at MidwestOne Bank in Fairfield, Ed Malloy (Mayor of Fairfield), Haresh Melwani, Dave Neff, Curtis Nelson, June and Lincoln Norton, Chelsey Owen and the whole Chelsey Henry gang, Mitchell and Renee Posner, Dennis Raimondi, M.E. Reich, Jeff Ring, Mark Rittmanic, Coral Rose, Marci Shimoff, Kent Sovern (Executive Director of the Des Moines Higher Education Collaborative), Ron Stakland, John Steuart, Carl Stone, Don Strauss, Robert Truog, Dean Vittitoe, Lila Wallace, Lee and Anita Warner, Warren Wechsler, Lisa Westercamp, Rosie Witherspoon, Richard Wong, my wonderful Aunt Sue Wolf, and Uncle Harry Hoffman.

Index

accounts payable, 10-12, 70–75, 225-230
accounts receivable, 225-230
advertising, 13–14, 236
anger, 196–197, 201, 208-209
apologies, 151, 157, 158, 220-221
appreciation, 20, 154, 174
approach, xv, xxi, 178, 192-199, 213. *See also* listening
arbitrator, 156-157
attachment, 75-77, 77-80, 142, 145, 199-202
attention, 236

banker, 102
bankruptcy, 11, 12, 225-226, 236
BATNA (Best Alternative To a Negotiated Agreement), 83–88
behavior, 70, 108-110, 238-240
best offer, 115-116
buyouts, 212-217

call centers, 81-82, 167–174
cash flow, 226-230
change, xiv-xv
Chapter 11, 236
collections, contract, 221–225
comfort zone, 6-9, 19, 37, 41
common ground, 4-8
communication, 2-4, 29-30, 66, 167-174, 180, 194, 204-205
compassion, 174
compliment, 20, 153-154
compromise, 212-214
contracts, xxii, 20–26, 35-37, 44-49, 100-101, 111-113, 148-149, 149-151,
    154-155, 156, 157, 158-160 177, 186-192, 218-225, 229, 230-231, 232-
    243. *See also* real estate
contract collections, 221-225

control. *See also* attachment; orange ball
59, 80-82, 156, 204
creativity, 175–176
credibility, 200

deal-breakers, 202–205
debt restructuring, 225–230

ego, 63–65, 139-140, 152, 177-179
emotions, 98-100, 151-152, 155-156, 173, 194, 238-239

fairness, 10, 12, 15, 116
finger-pointing, 142-143
flexibility, 62-63
friends, xxiv-xxv, 117-118, 151, 237-241

giving in, 31–32
goals, xxii, 1–2, 46, 206-208
good cop/bad cop, 80–82
greed, 67

history, 46-47, 95-97, 100-101, 111-113
honesty, 65-66, 67-69, 158, 184-192. *See also* spin, of truth
humility, 93-94, 118-120, 160
humor, 23, 105-111, 182, 194, 171, 220

integrity, xxii–xxiv. *See also* honesty
involvement, 37-38
issues, 167–174

lawyers, xiv, xxii, 9, 20, 23–24, 39–41, 47–49, 113-115, 131-138, 141, 148,
     156, 161-164
leases, 2-3, 26–29, 85-88, 100-101, 157, 177, 212-217
listening, 98-99, 111-113, 127-128, 194, 181, 217
lying, 68-69. *See also* spin, of truth

marriage, 231-232
money, 10–12, 13–15, 125-126, 173. *See also* specific renegotiations

negotiation, renegotiation vs., xv, xxiii, 80, 95, 123
niceness, 101–103, 194, 231
no, 26, 207-208

offer, best, 117–118
orange ball, 51–55, 95. *See also* specific renegotiations

patience, 89-91, 180, 183, 207
persistence, 183, 208
personal contracts, 230–231, 232-233, 233-237, 237-242
preparation, 118-121
production, international, 126, 158-160, 195-199, 219-221
public offering, 39–42

questions, 30–31, 38, 56, 180

real estate, 70–75, 85-88, 100-101, 157, 176, 184, 208-209, 212-217
renegotiating
action points, 43
checklist, 42–51
definition, xxi
fundamentals, xiv, 166
negotiation vs., xv, xxiii, 80, 95, 123
preparation points, 42
principles, xvii
reasons for, 38
with right person, 19–26, 154-155
right person for, 45, 139-142, 152-153, 158-160, 164
stages, 4–6
with yourself, 33-34, 88-89, 115-117
renegotiator, professional, xx, 141–142, 163
rentals, 15-17, 85-88, 100-101, 157, 176-177, 203
reputation, 69, 91, 162-163, 196-198, 220
respect, xxi, xxii, 65
retail, 13–14, 185-186
rightness, 15–18

settlement, 5–6, 8, 10, 32–33, 34–37
silence, 98-99, 110, 129-131. *See also* listening
simplicity, 127
spin, of truth, 1–4, 61-62, 67
stories
    art dealers, 186–192
    athletes, 35-37
    bad baskets, 158-160
    car rentals, 15–17
    Coffee Imports International, 3, 75-77, 118-121, 129-131

construction site, 223-225
contractor, 113-115
customs officials, 55-59, 105-111, 149-151
department stores, 12-14
dolls, defective, 149-151
equipment lease, 26-29
gift sets, 195-199
grandmother, 233-237
hotel rates, 6–8, 9
imports, 55-59, 89-91, 105-111, 126, 149-151, 158-160, 195-199
jewelry purchase, 32–33
Mypoints, xxiv-xxv, 218
photo company, 67
Pick 'n' Save, 77-79
plush toys, 126
restaurant, Tru, 181-183
software contract, 20-26
Storage Networks, xxiv-xxv
stuffed animals, 18–19
subcontractors, international, 89-91
telecom, 10-12, 20-26, 39-41, 44-49, 132-135, 144-148, 146-148, 154-155
United Call, 81-82
USA Global Link, 39-41, 44-49, 85-88
Zimmerman, Bill, 77-79

stress, xxv, 104

talking, 29-30
techniques, control, 95
Transcendental Meditation program (TM), 104

venting, 97-98, 99, 180

wholesale, 12-14, 118-120, 126, 129-131,149-151
winning, 60–62
women, 22, 55-59, 58–61, 103, 150-152, 168-172, 208-209, 217, 220-221

Marc Freeman is now consulting, speaking, and giving workshops on Renegotiating with Integrity. He has created the following topics for key-note speachs, half day, and full day workshops. Company-specific topics available upon request.

Renegotiating with Integrity: It's Not Just Business, It's Personal
This speech defines the difference between negotiating and renegotiating. Marc describes his five principles through stories from his business and personal life.

Renegotiating with Employees and Business Partners
Integrating a new employee or business partner into your company is all about the skills of Renegotiating. This presentation gives participants the perspective of both sides to successfully prepare for this event.

Renegotiating Your Corporate Culture: A New Strategy for a New Millennium
Corporate cultures are difficult to control and even more difficult to maintain. In today's business environment, it has been proven that if the corporate culture is one of integrity, where employees are both expected and encouraged to treat each other and their customers with respect and honesty, your bottom line will be affected in a positive way. This presentation gives management and human resource personnel the skills necessary to create that culture.

Renegotiating Skills for Women
Women find themselves renegotiating more than most men in both their personal and professional lives. Because most women are juggling two roles they need to be prepared to Renegotiate with Integrity. Marc's principles for renegotiating will give women the ability to keep their integrity while achieving their goals.

Renegotiating Skills for Sales Personnel
Having managed and trained over 4,000 sales people worldwide, Marc has a unique perspective on what a complete sale involves. Through his "Sales Timeline" he explains how and when sales people need to renegotiate with their customers. Marc gives specific techniques to create better relationships not only with customers but also internally, with other divisions of the company.

Renegotiating Skills for Customer Service Associates
No one Renegotiates more that those in the field of customer service. Every call they take is a Renegotiation. Marc's principles and techniques will upgrade your customer service department as well as reduce the stress for your associates.

Renegotiate Your Happiness
This inspirational speech gives the audience the skills to take control of their own lives. Marc will inspire them with the realization that there is no barrier to being happy. This is a powerful, humorous, uplifting, and creative presentation.

Marc Freeman & Associates
www.renegotiate.tv

641 / 472 - 2727 office
641 / 472 - 2151 fax
917 / 669 - 7251 cell

Marc Freeman
& Associates

Book Order Form
Renegotiate with Integrity
It's Not Business, It's Personal

PO Box 2200 • Fairfield, Iowa, USA 52556 • 641-472-2727 • www.renegotiate.tv

Date: _____   Gift: ☐ YES ☐ NO

Name of Company: _____

Name of Contact: _____   Title of Contact: _____

Phone: _____   Fax: _____

Email: _____   Purchase Order No. (if required): _____

Billing Address   **Shipping Address**

Name:	Name:
Company:	Company:
Address:	Address:
Phone:	Phone:

Order: *Renegotiate with Integrity*   **Quantity**   **Price**

Fewer than 10 copies $20/book   _____   _____

10 to 99 copies $18/book   _____   _____

100 or more copies $16/book   _____   _____

Tax Exempt No.: _____   Subtotal _____

Promotional Code: _____   Shipping _____

Tax (7%) _____

Please allow 45 days for delivery. Non-returnable.

Total _____

Payment Method: ☐ cash   ☐ check   ☐ Visa   ☐ MasterCard   ☐ American Express

Credit Card Account Number: _____

Name as it appears on the card: _____

Credit Card Authorized Signature: _____

Customer Signature: _____

Organization: _____

Printed in the United States
93660LV00001B/7-64/A

9 781427 608529